mag

Modelling RAF Vehicles

Gerald Scarborough

AIRFIX PSL

Patrick Stephens Ltd
in association with Airfix Products Ltd

First published—1978

ISBN 0 85059 261 5

Cover design by Tim McPhee

Text set in 8 on 9 pt Univers Medium by Stevenage Printing Limited, Stevenage.
Printed in Great Britain on Fineblade cartridge 90 gsm and bound by the Garden City Press, Letchworth, Herts.
Published by Patrick Stephens Limited, Bar Hill, Cambridge, CB3 8EL, in association with Airfix Products Limited, London SW18.

Don't forget these other Airfix Magazine Guides!

Contents

Editor's introduction

It is a genuine delight to watch an expert at work, and always therefore a pleasure to introduce a new modelling title by Gerald Scarborough. Unfortunately this will be his last in this series, as this is the penultimate *Airfix Magazine Guide*, but many people will consider it his best, and certainly his most original. Military vehicle modellers have been well served, not only in this series of books but also in magazine articles, etc, but not so the thousands who like creating dioramas depicting wartime airfield activity.

Fortunately there is a ready source of material for conversions and scratch-builds in the three Airfix airfield sets, the Recovery, Refuelling and Emergency kits, especially now a Morris Commercial and Bofors have been added to the range. However, there are still numerous gaps, ranging from staff cars, crew buses and runway caravans to searchlights, balloon winches and armoured cars. The intention of this book was to fill some of those vital gaps, and Gerald has excelled himself with this collection.

The text has deliberately been kept to a minimum in order to include the greatest possible number of drawings and photographs, but the basic modelling techniques should be familiar to anyone who has read one or more of Gerald's previous books in this series (No 1 *Plastic Modelling*, No 3 *Military Modelling*, No 5 *Tank & AFV Modelling* and No 21 *Modelling Armoured Cars*). Further information on the wheeled vehicles used by the RFC/RAF can be found in Bruce Robertson's series of article which began in the October 1977 issue of *Airfix Magazine*.

The modelling examples in this book range from very simple conversions of existing Airfix kits to fairly complicated scratch-builds which will require some modelling experience to complete—including a 1:76 scale barrage balloon! But none of them should be beyond the average modeller with a few conversions beneath his belt, and for aircraft modellers in particular they offer a refreshing diversion. Hopefully, through reading this book, some aircraft modellers will discover that vehicles aren't so boring as they had always thought, and similarly many military vehicle modellers may feel they ought to 'have a go' at an aircraft for a change. Variety *is* the spice of life, and the old maxim applies just as much to modelling as to any other activity. In any case, it's a good selection of interesting, entertaining and challenging models, so have fun!

BRUCE QUARRIE

one

Tools, materials and techniques

The Airfix range of RAF vehicle kits, the Emergency set, Refuelling set and Recovery set, have been popular as accessories to airfield scene dioramas since their introduction. They also, together with other vehicle kits in the Airfix range, serve as a basis for converting and scratch-building a host of other military vehicles.

The object of this book is to provide ideas and data, especially drawings and sketches, showing how these models can be made. Research for this book revealed that there was no hope of including all the vehicles used by the Royal Air Force so some strict pruning was required and coverage was limited to the more popular for the most part, but with some rarer types included to try to cover as many aspects as possible of this subject. Of course, a lot of the types were used by the Army as well as the Air Force and I trust that this book will appeal also to the 'grounded' modellers as well as the flying types.

While the main bulk of subjects covered will be World War 2 orientated, there are several types from the early days, 1914-1918 and the between-the-wars period.

It is difficult to classify all the vehicles to any particular period as several World War 2 types were still in use up to the late 1960s along with their more modern replacements so I shall first deal with straight conversions from the Airfix kits and then continue with scratch-built projects from the 1914-1918 period up to 1939, followed by scratch-builds from the World War 2 period. This is a rather arbitrary split as again there must be some overlap of intention as some scratch-builds will be more complex conversions but basically, to me, a scratch-build is one using few kit parts, ie, wheels, axles, etc, whereas a conversion uses chassis, cab, wheels, axles, etc.

As additions to the airfield scene there are, of course, the Airfix control tower kit, the RAF personnel sets and others that can be adapted, such as the figures in the vehicle sets and other military kits, lots of which can be pressed into service on an airfield scene.

Only a few tools will be required for all the models described, in fact very few more than you would need to build any plastic kit. A craft knife; a steel rule as a guide to cutting and also of course for measuring and marking out; a pair of tweezers; a pair of geometry compasses for scoring planks, or some other sharp pointed tool, for example an old dart; a fine drill (1/16 inch diameter) in a pin chuck; a razor saw or six-inch Junior hacksaw; and a few files, sandpaper, manicure scissors, pins, Sellotape, etc, but no doubt you have got your own favourite tools and techniques which you have also evolved.

Plasticard, Rikokard or Polycard, whatever they call your favourite sheet plastic in 10, 20, 30 40 and 60 thou thicknessess, plastic rod and Microstrip or Rikostrip and adhesive are basically all you will need in the way of materials, together with your usual bits-box which should contain all the unused parts from every kit you have ever made—I can promise you if you make all the models covered by this book, then you will have a fair stock of spares to add to your collection—and, I hope, a fine collection of RAF vehicle models.

Beginners to the hobby will find some of the basic techniques described more fully in some of the earlier books in this series so I will not waste a lot of space going over old ground again—as we come to each model I will describe any particular aspect that I think may be helpful.

Probably the most useful books to have by you for reference are the *Observer's Army Vehicles Directory to 1940, The Observer's Fighting Vehicles*

Directory World War 2 and the *Observer's Military Vehicles Directory from 1945*, all compiled by Bart H. Vanderveen. These three volumes cover not only British vehicles but are essential references to the general picture of the types of military soft skin used in the periods covered. Canadian and American vehicles were also used by the RAF and these also you will find mentioned in Vanderveen's trio of directories.

If your favourite vehicle is not to be found or cannot be adapted from the drawings in this book then John Church of 'Honeywood', Middle Road, Tiptoe, Lymington, Hants, has a very extensive list of drawings which are very reasonably priced and I suggest a line to John, with a stamped addressed envelope, will be well worth while.

My thanks especially to John for help with material and information for this book, also to Peter Green who is so often surprising me with photographs he has discovered, to Neville Franklin who has now learnt to point his camera at vehicles as well as aircraft, to Terry Gander for the loan of some negatives, to the Shuttleworth Trust and many military vehicle enthusiasts for answering my eternal questions and allowing me to photograph and measure their vehicles, and to anyone else who may have helped without knowing with a tip or some other information.

two

Simple conversions

One of the most useful kits to be produced for the RAF and military modeller is the RAF Emergency set because the two Austins it contains appeared in so many guises and with a multitude of bodies. I confess I have not yet had time to make up the standard crash tender as supplied in the kit because I have had so much enjoyment converting it to other vehicles—one day, perhaps, I'll make it as it should be!

This Austin K6 chassis was used for many bodies, some of which are drawn here. Photographs are particularly helpful in establishing detail fitting for each and generally the chassis can be assembled as Section 4 of the kit instruction leaflet, but cut away the continuation of the running boards along the fuel tank on the nearside and round off the lower edge of the tank. The bonnet/cab assembly, parts 23 to 34, can be cemented in place to the chassis. Note on some models the hip ring may not be fitted in which case, of course, fill with scrap and body putty and smooth to shape.

Bomb flat

This was used to transport bombs up to 1,000 lbs or gas cylinders for balloon barrages, and could tow a loaded trailer of up to four tons weight. The Bomb flat body is simple using a basic 40 thou plastic card scored to represent the planking with the short drop sides of 30 thou plastic card and the hinge irons from Microstrip. Note the POW (Petrol, Oil or Water) carriers fitted at the rear.

Fire tender CO_2

This carries four banks of six 60 lb CO_2 cylinders and two trolley mounted 25 lb CO_2 cylinders and the model makes an ideal companion to the Airfix crash tender.

The two portable cylinders stowed

Bedford QL 4 × 4 GS truck.

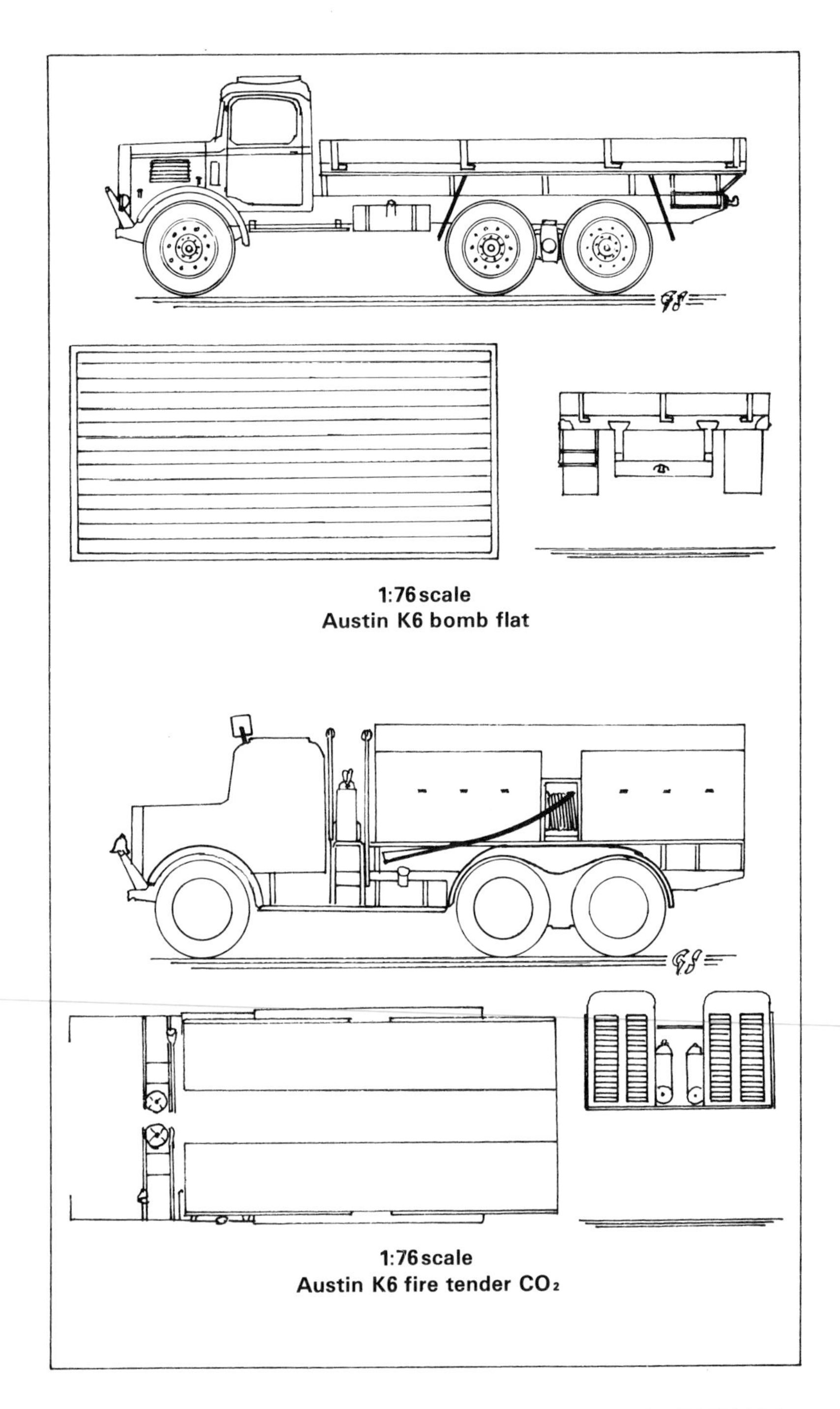

1:76 scale
Austin K6 bomb flat

1:76 scale
Austin K6 fire tender CO_2

behind the cab are removed down the folding ramps each side. Construction is basically a series of boxes although wood could be used for the cylinder bank containers with the side access panels from 10 thou plastic card. The top, with its rounded edges, can be from laminations of plastic card filed to shape. The hose reels come from the kit (part 60) and there are, in fact, three, one each side and one at the rear on the nearside. Note the rear mudguards—the between-axles section is re-shaped and they are cut away from the main central 'box' and cemented underneath the platform individually. Some models did not have the hip-ring in the cab roof.

Aircrew coach

A familiar sight on wartime airfields to transport aircrew to dispersal, the body of this vehicle was fitted with longitudinal seats and luggage racks. Often driven with doors open, this could well be featured in a diorama depicting the 'off on a mission' situation. Construction is just a box but use at least 30 thou plastic card to avoid warping, cut out and glaze the windows and build up the roof from laminations of plastic card and file and sand to shape. This body was also fitted to the Ford WOT-1 chassis, for which see a later section.

Coles Mk VII 6.3-ton crane

You may find that parts from the Airfix Recovery set crane can be used for this but it is probably easier to scratch-build. The turntable is built up from discs of thick plastic card to which the floor section and the super-structure are added as shown on the sketch. The jib can be made from 20 thou thick Microstrip, building up each side and then adding the cross section much as you may have built flying model aircraft. I have made larger jibs than this from Plastruct angle section but I think that

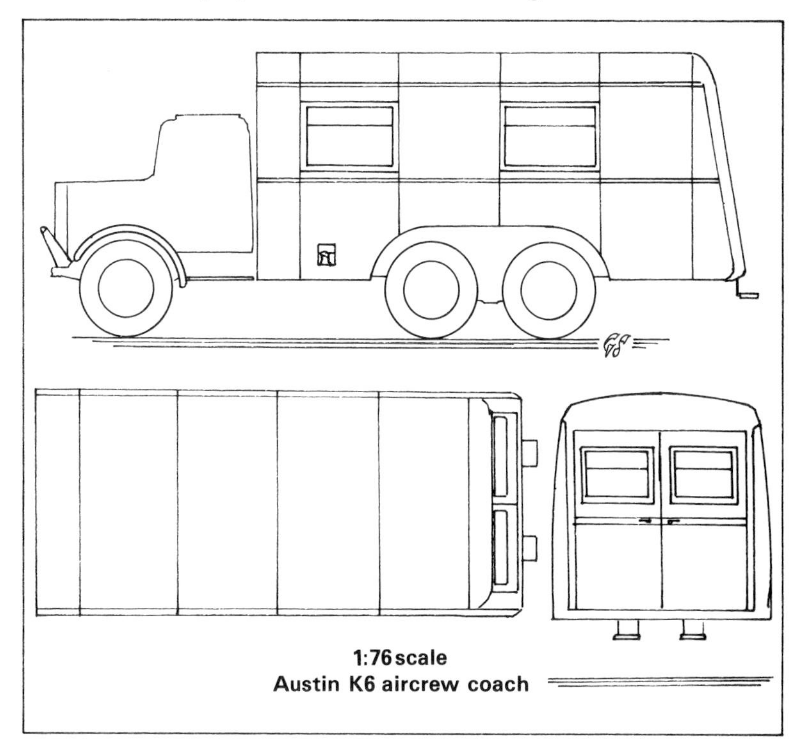

1:76 scale
Austin K6 aircrew coach

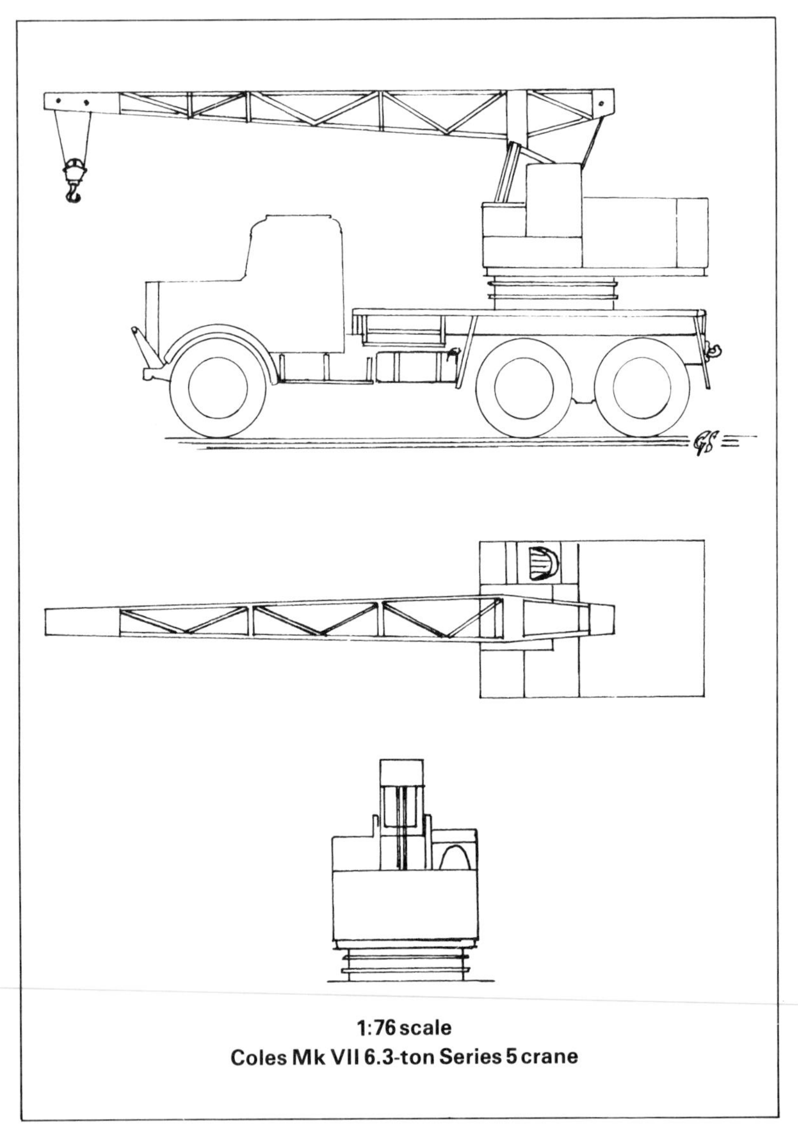

1:76 scale
Coles Mk VII 6.3-ton Series 5 crane

for a small one like this, Microstrip is quite satisfactory. The platform on which the whole crane sits is 30 thou plastic card with two runners between it and the chassis cut from 40 thou plastic card. This crane was also fitted to Ford WOT-1, Crossley IGL8 and Leyland Retriever chassis.

This by no means exhausts the Austin K6 version as there were many breakdown gantry, wireless, office and similar 'house-type' bodies fitted. Two of these and an Austin K3/YF were described in *Airfix Magazine Guide 3—Military Modelling*.

Austin K2 30 cwt 4 × 2 GS

The GS truck version of the Austin K2

Thornycroft / Amazon WF/AC6/1 with Coles Mk VII crane.

Thornycroft Amazon WF8/AC6/2 with Coles crane.

30 cwt 4 × 2 is a simple conversion from the ambulance in the kit. Build up the chassis as the kit instructions but cut away the ambulance body floor to leave just the front driver's compartment. Cut away the windscreen and fit together the remaining firewall (part 37) and the radiator and bonnet to the front mudguards and chassis assembly. Cut out the cab rear from 30 thou plastic card and make up the hood from tissue paper, covering a 20 thou plastic card base as per the sketch.

Canvas doors can be added either in place or rolled forward to the firewall edges. The body is from 20 or 30 thou plastic card, scored clearly to represent the planking and with bearers under-

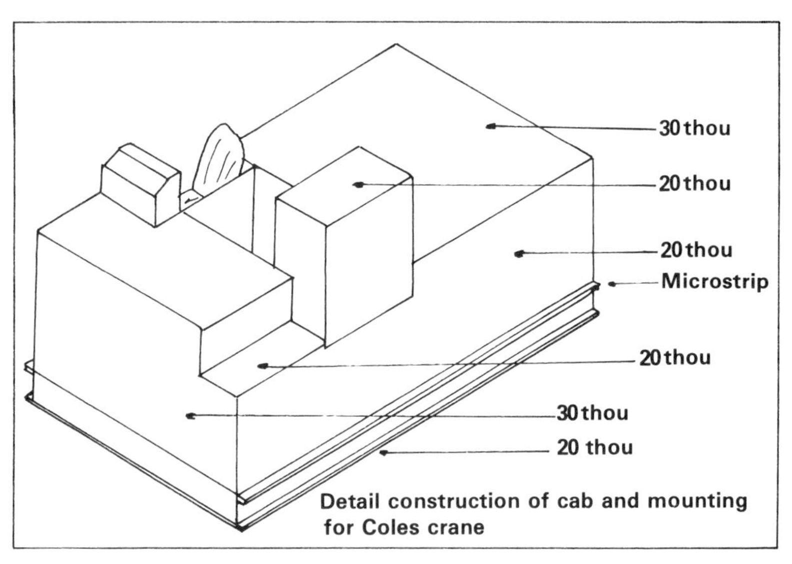

Detail construction of cab and mounting for Coles crane

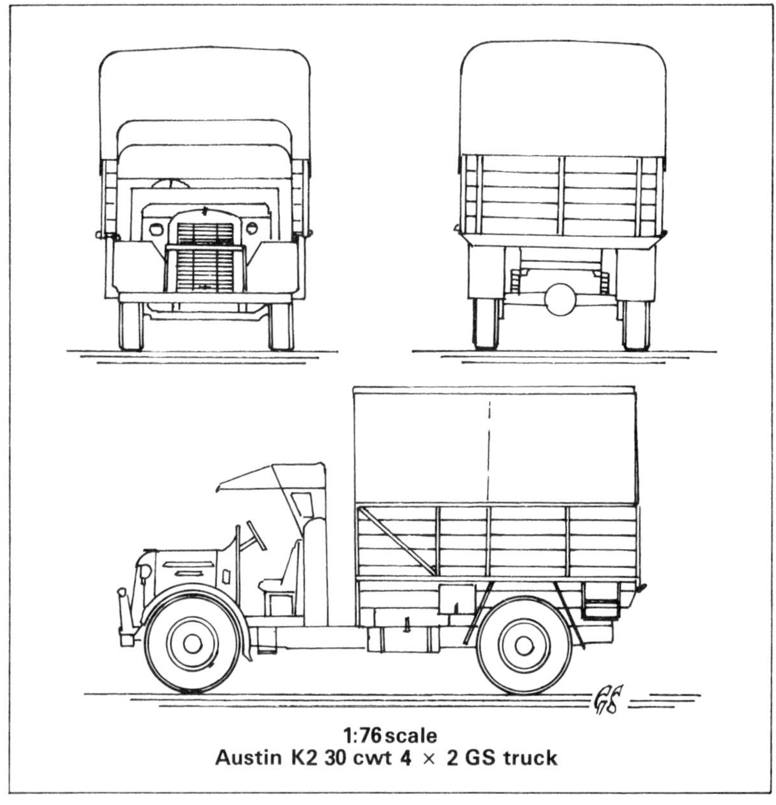
1:76 scale
Austin K2 30 cwt 4 × 2 GS truck

neath to space it from the chassis frame. The tilt frame can be added from thin plastic rod and covered with tissue paper. A spare wheel is stowed between the cab and the body on the offside.

Austin K2 3-ton 4 × 2 GS

The drawings show the 3-ton steel-bodied Austin fitted with 10.50 × 16 tyres and closed cab. Early versions are as the previous model with open cab but with 34 × 7 tyres and twin wheels at the rear. The version can be modelled from a combination of parts from the two kits using the cab from the K6 and the bonnet from the K2 with the body scratch-built as usual. Note the chassis will have to be extended by 8mm.

RAF Refuelling set—Bedford QLR/QLD/QLT

The most popular of the two vehicles in this kit is the Bedford QL as this chassis was used for so many types and in fact, they are still to be seen in civilian use today.

The drawings illustrate three types of body, a wireless 'house-type', a General Service truck and the troop or personnel carrier. Note how on all three the rear wheel arch extends up into the body of the vehicle so that on the open truck an internal box has to built up. On the QLT this forms part of the side seating arrangement. They were usually to be seen with the tilt sides rolled up and fastened along the top edge of the 'roof'. Note the double opening doors in the tail and the doors in the sides at the front. This makes another good model for taking crew to the aircraft, a role it would often fulfil.

The QLR 'house-type' is again basically a box with rounded top corners. The details of doors and grilles can be added from 5 thou plastic card, scored lightly as required, and the window apertures should be glazed inside the body with clear plastic card. You will find it easier to glaze the windows if either the top or, preferably, the floor of the body are left out until the model has been painted inside and out. The clear plastic card can then be cemented inside without any fear of splodging it with paint at a later stage.

The cab of the Bedford can be improved by fitting a steering wheel and by carving away inside the mudguards so that the edges appear thinner.

The AEC refueller in this kit has very little conversion potential although its chassis parts, wheels, axles, etc, are very useful when scratch-building some of the larger army vehicles. The chassis was used as a mobile crane and this was described in *Airfix Guide 3—Military Modelling*. This is a simple mating of the Coles crane from the recovery set allied to the AEC chassis.

Recovery set—Queen Mary semi-trailer

I think the first thing to do is to overcome the shortcomings of the Queen Mary semi-trailer as supplied in the kit. My drawings were based on the preserved trailer at Newark Air Museum, the only alteration to which has been to the swan-neck turntable plate and the fitting of modern lights and reflectors to conform to current legislation.

To alter the Airfix model cut away some of the diagonal bracing strips from the outer side members (parts 39 and 41) to correspond to the drawings. The

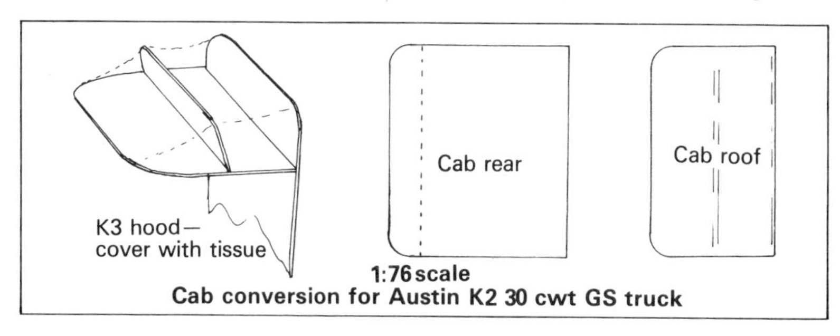

1:76 scale
Cab conversion for Austin K2 30 cwt GS truck

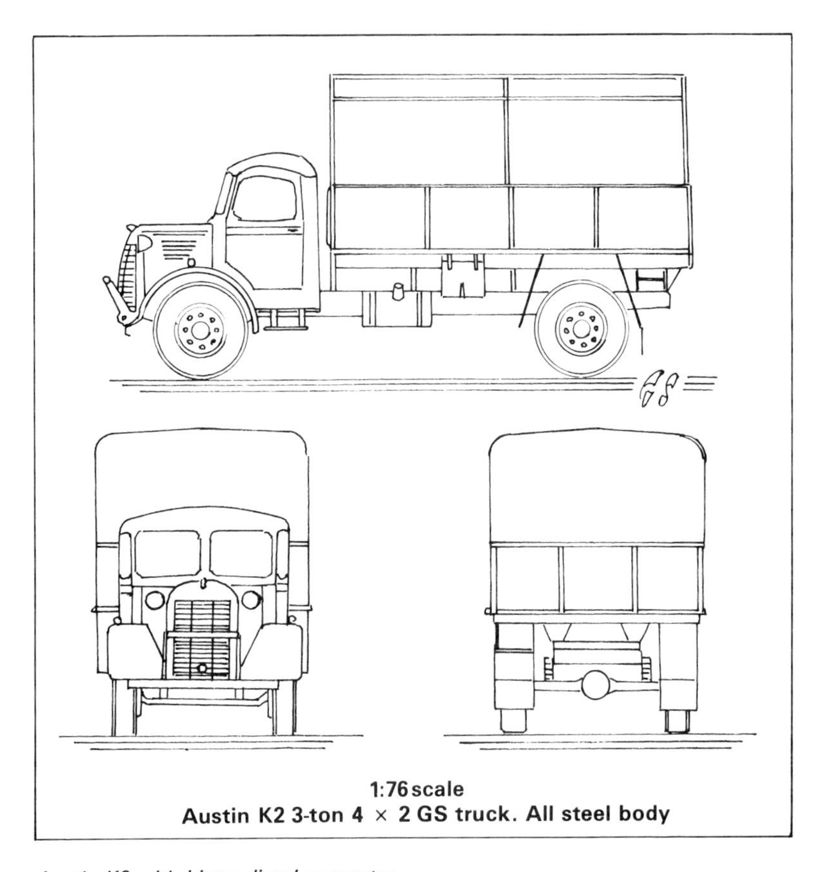

Austin K6 with Lister diesel generator.

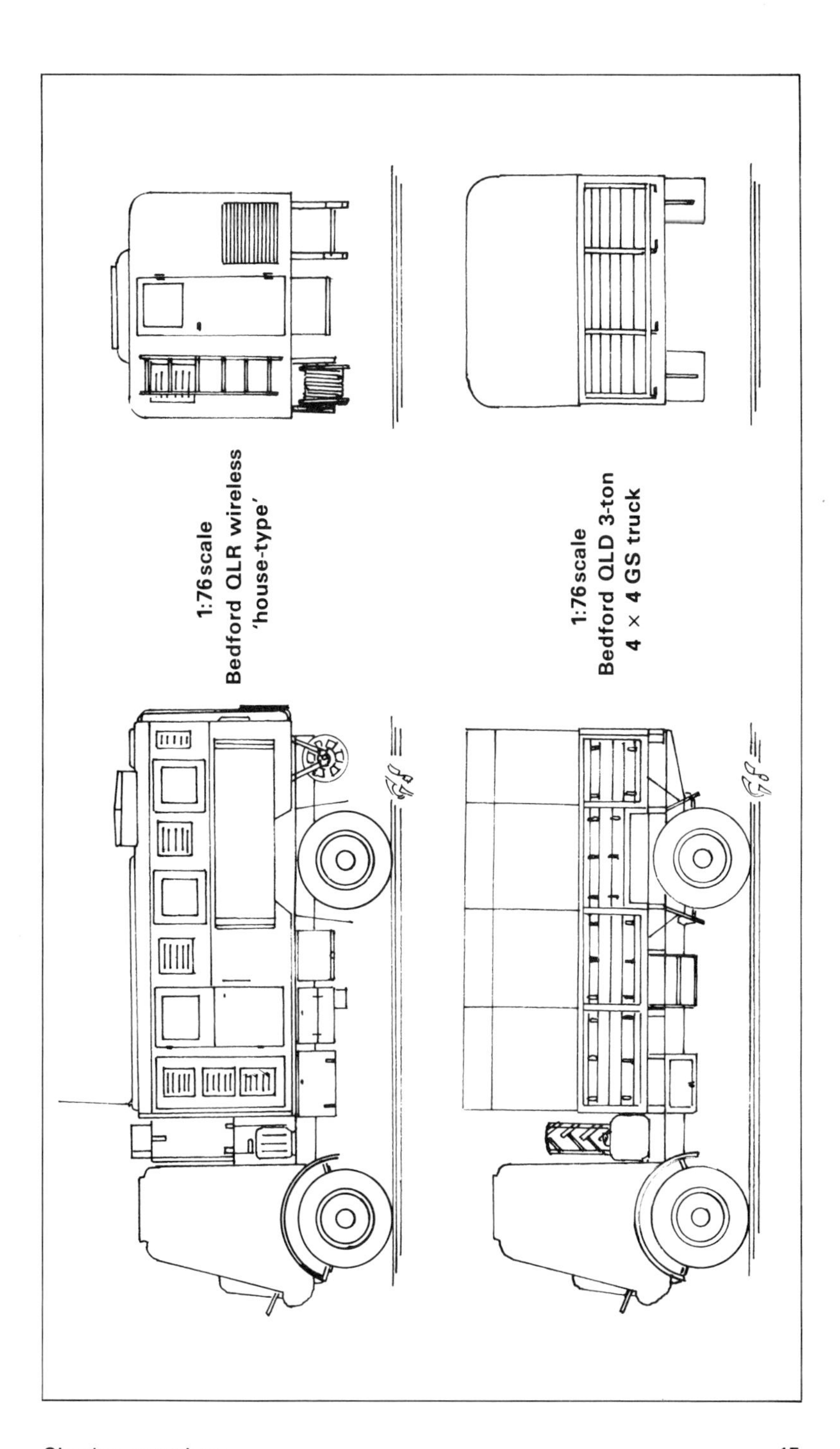
1:76 scale
Bedford QLR wireless
'house-type'
1:76 scale
Bedford QLD 3-ton
4 × 4 GS truck

View of side bracing on preserved trailer.

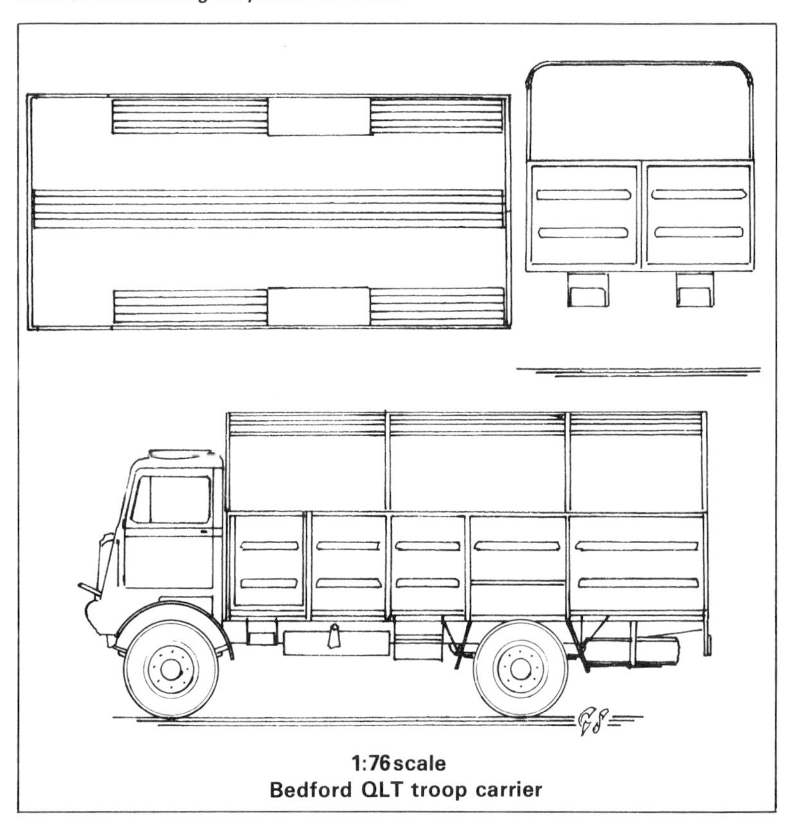

1:76 scale
Bedford QLT troop carrier

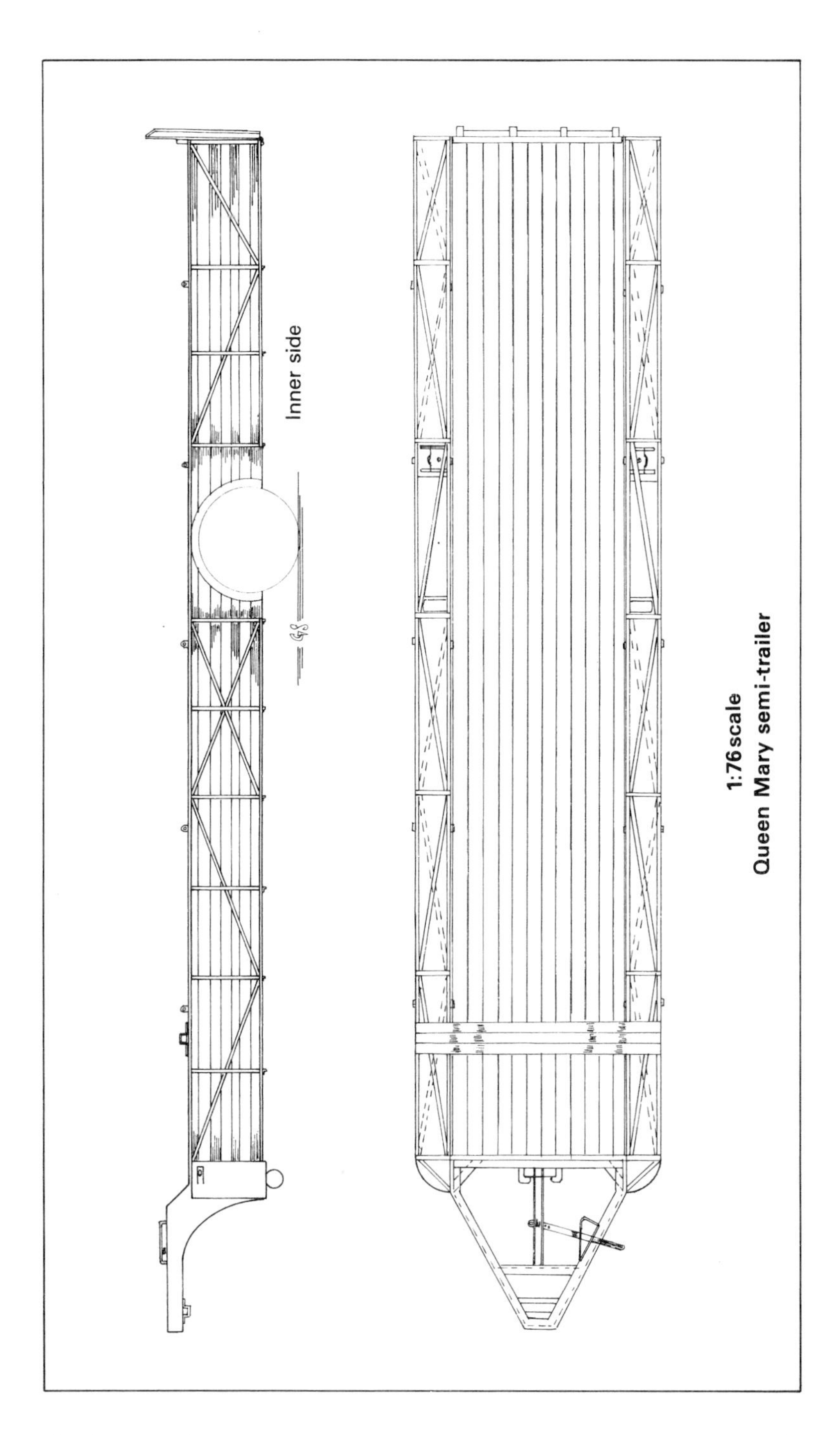
Inner side
1:76 scale
Queen Mary semi-trailer

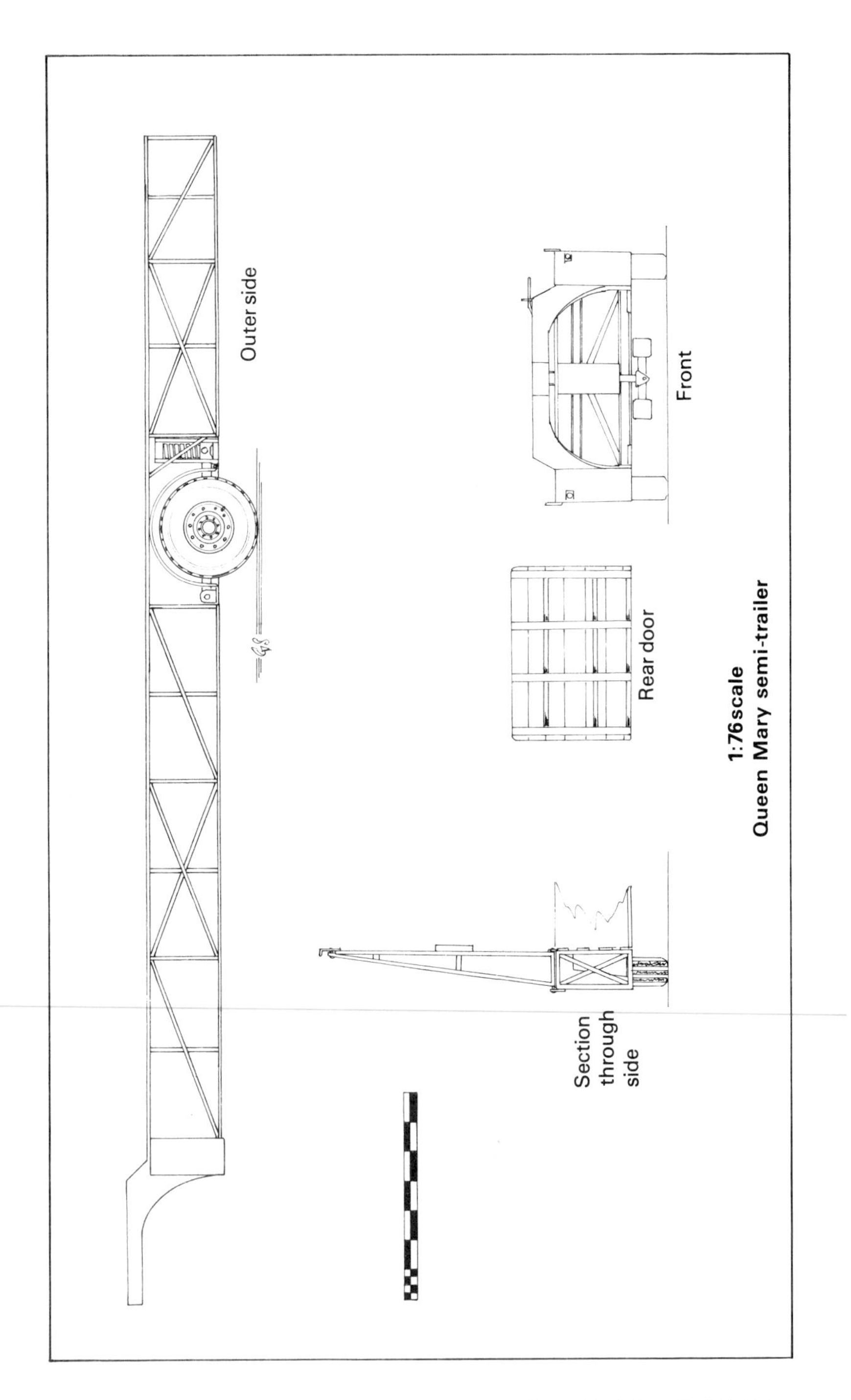

1:76 scale
Queen Mary semi-trailer

Above *Detail of fuselage support beam fitted to Queen Mary semi-trailer.*

Right *Commer Q2 tractor unit with Queen Mary semi-trailer followed by Crossley Q type and a second Commer with flat semi-trailer.*

Right *The swan-neck on the preserved trailer at Newark Museum.*

Below *Side view of a Queen Mary semi-trailer.*

Above *Bedford MWC 4 × 2 water tanker.* **Left** *Close up detail of spare wheel carrier and plumbing.* **Below** *Rear view of Bedford MWC.*

inner and outer side members are cemented together with solid joining pieces moulded into each half and unfortunately the joins will show all along the top. This can be disguised by cutting away a small piece at the top of each and over-laying this with short Microstrip cut to length. Before

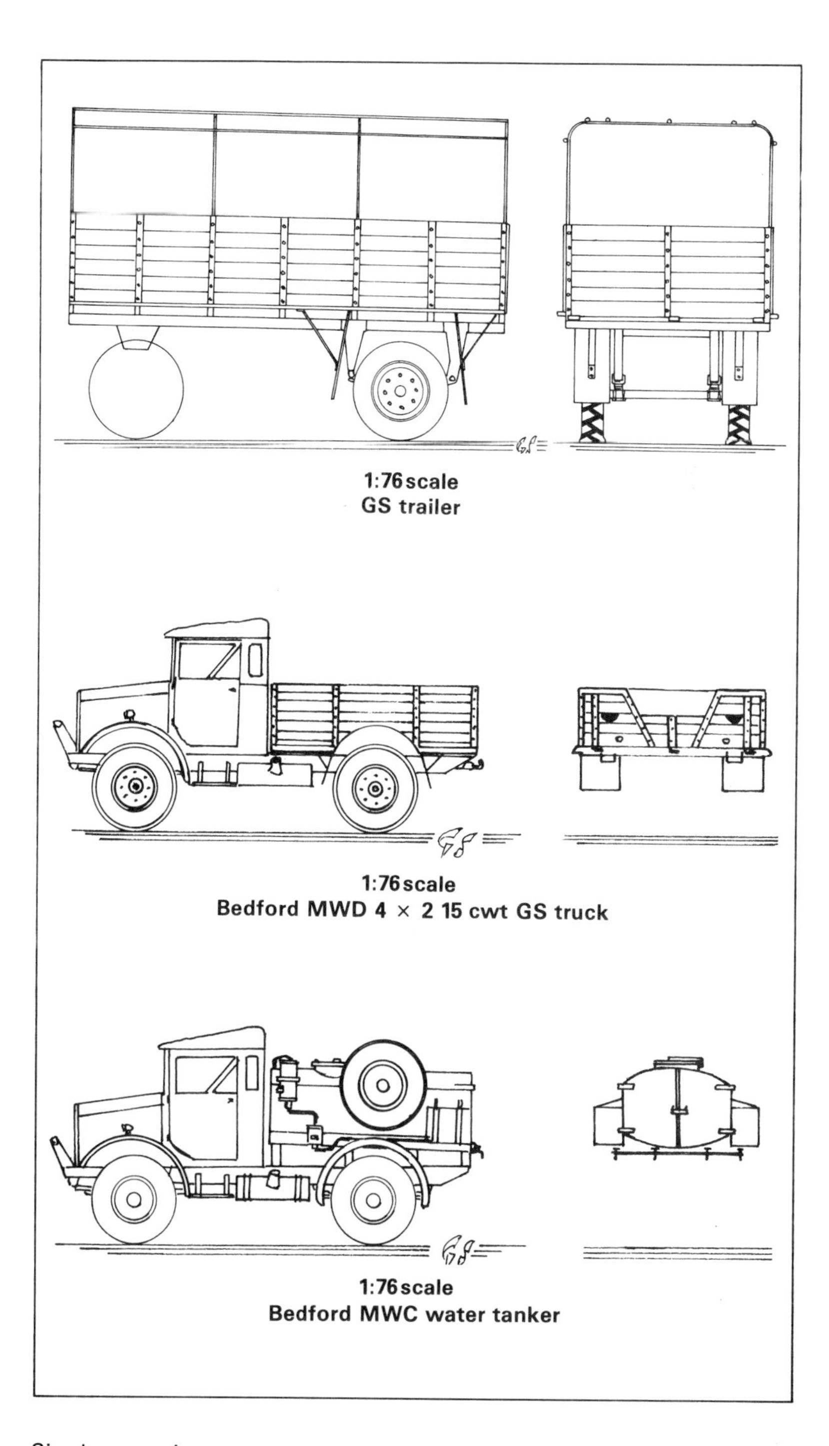

1:76 scale
GS trailer

1:76 scale
Bedford MWD 4 × 2 15 cwt GS truck

1:76 scale
Bedford MWC water tanker

Bedford MWD GS truck. Compare bonnet side panel grilles with Bedford MWC (Terry Gander).

cementing the pairs of side frames together add the diagonal bracing strips to the inner side pieces, again as shown on the drawings.

The swan-neck (part 44) should also be altered by cutting away the sloping sides (where the decal 'MAX LOAD goes) at right angles to the front. The photographs and sketch show where the corners should be curved plates. The floor, side frames and front can now be assembled. Cement in place the diagonal bracing strips between the side frame halves and the cross brace at the rear end. 10 thou plastic card is used to cover the gaps left each side of the swan-neck and then the curved plates and small diagonal angle iron braces can be cemented in place.

To further detail the trailer, build a set of front legs and wheels to go under the swan-neck and also add the additional cross bracing to the front. Most pictures of Queen Mary trailers I have seen show it equipped with hinged side extensions and these should be made up from thin Microstrip and cemented in place.

GS trailer

A simple GS trailer drawing is also included as an alternative for use with the Bedford tractor unit. The Bedford tractor unit can be used as a basis for many of the innumerable Bedford types used. There are one or two alterations I usually make to the kit, the first being to use front mudguards cut from the Austin in the Emergency set or to mould new ones from plastic card. This is more important for the OY types but also improves the MW range. Another is to increase the thickness of the wheels by filing the inside faces flat and cementing a disc of 15 thou plastic card in between each half.

Bedford MWD

The MWD 4 × 2 15 cwt GS truck hardly needs more than the wheels, chassis and axles from the kit but less experienced modellers may like to use the bonnet parts as well. First job then is to cut a section out of the chassis frame, just behind the tank supports and in

Bedford OY petrol bowser. Note extended rear of cab.

front of the rear-spring hangers. Cement the two parts together squarely and allow to dry to give the wheelbase as shown on the drawings. You will see that this version is fitted with an open-type cab, the new rear and sides/doors are from 15 or 20 thou plastic card with the hood built up and covered with tissue paper. The flat windscreen is from clear plastic card with the frame added from Microstrip. Drawings are included for the GS truck version and an MWC water tanker.

Bedford OYD 4 × 2 GS truck.

Bedford OXD

The Bedford OX and OY series were fitted with larger wheels than the MW series so new mudguards to the bonnet section are essential. The cab can be taken from the Recovery set with front mudguards from the Austin K6 in the Emergency set or moulded as usual by cutting strips of 20 thou plastic card, curving round a suitable size wooden dowel and holding in place with masking tape. Pour boiling water over to mould to shape then immerse in cold water to set the new shape. An alternative is to use the Austin K6 cab with a new bonnet from plastic card as the sketch. Don't forget to fill in the hip-ring in the cab roof. The chassis is easy to scratch-build using 40 thou plastic card and axles, springs and wheels come from the Emergency set.

Front view of Bedford OY—typical of Bedford cabs.

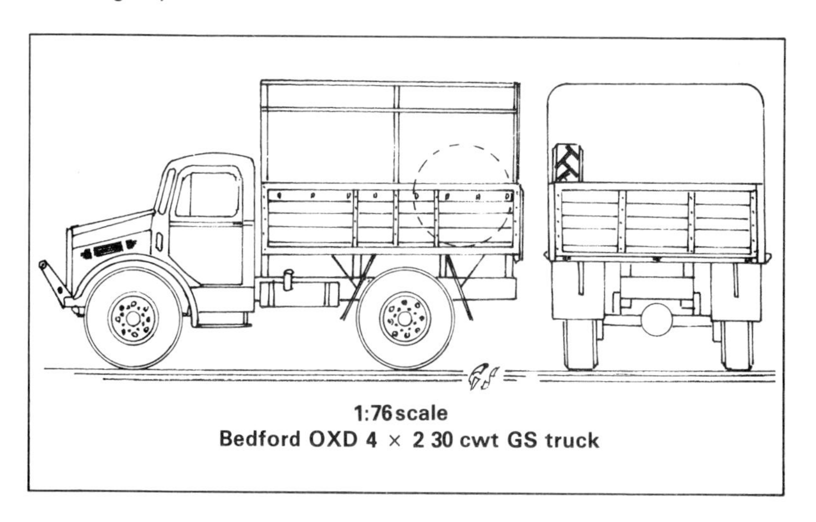

1:76 scale
Bedford OXD 4 × 2 30 cwt GS truck

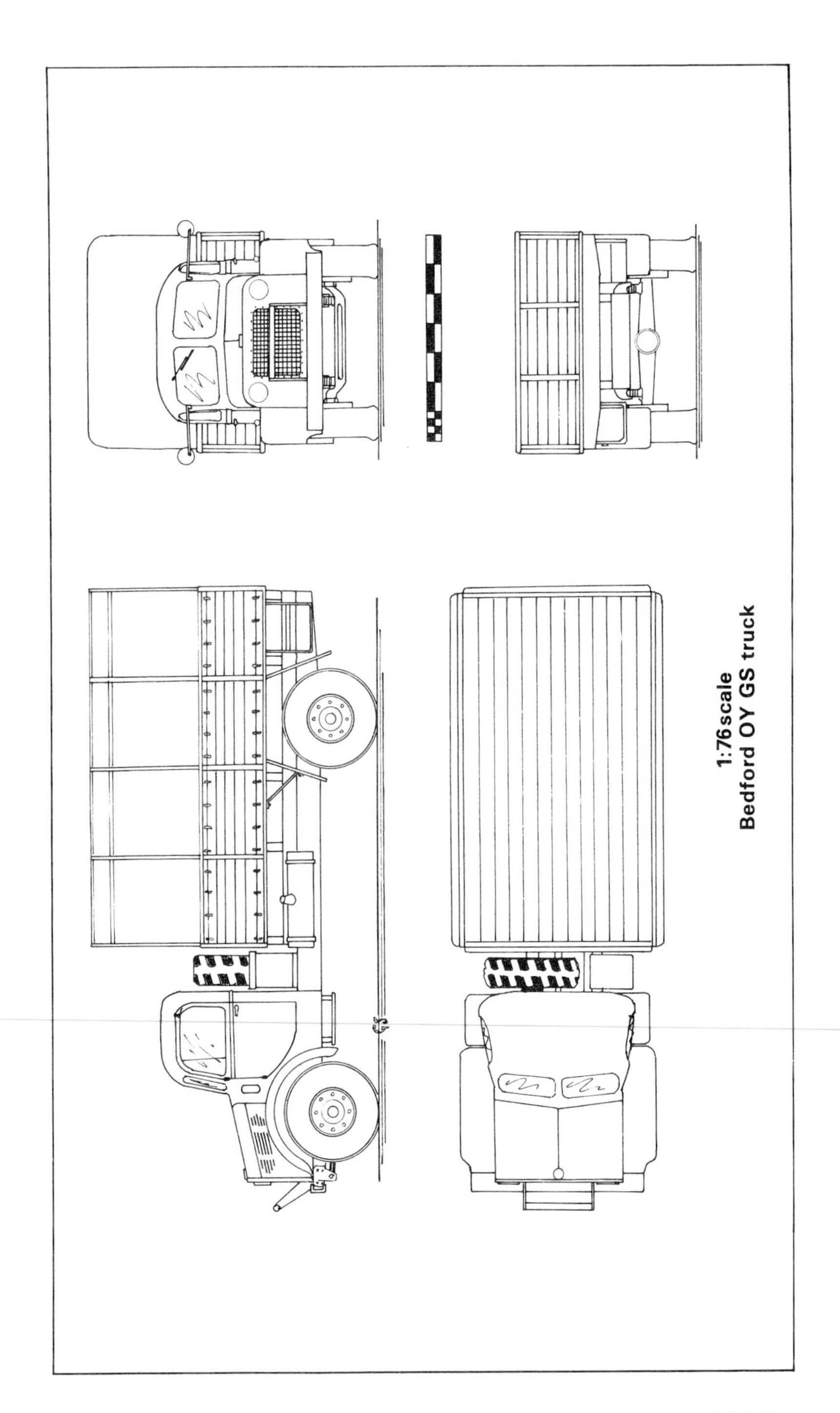
1:76 scale
Bedford OY GS truck

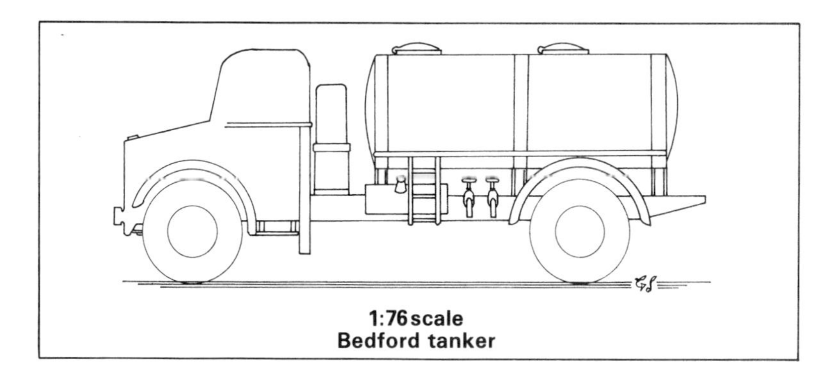

1:76 scale
Bedford tanker

Bedford OY

Construction of the OY is as for the OX and drawings are included for the OY GS and for the tanker versions. Note the tanker version has an extension below the rear of the cab. The tank for this is made by combining parts from two Bedford QL kits. The rear chassis of the Bedford QL can be combined with the front part of the Bedford tractor unit from the Recovery set but this is a bit expensive and I suggest scratch-building at least the rear chassis.

This by no means exhausts the number of Bedford conversions possible with Airfix kits as the MW, OX and OY series chassis were widely used. Additional drawings appear on John Church's list, in the various *Bellona Military Vehicle Data* booklets, and in *British Light Military Trucks 1939-1945*, by Mike Conniford, also published by Bellona.

Bofors gun and tractor—Morris CS8 GS truck

The Airfix Bofors gun kit, apart from its obvious deployment as airfield defence installations, provides the basis for many early Morris truck conversions. The cab section from this kit and a shortened chassis with scrapbox springs and one of the kit rear axles can form the basic ingredients for the Morris CS8. Drawings are included for the CS8 GS truck which is fitted with two aero screens in place of the flat windscreen in the kit and W/T van. Drawings for a C4 W/T van are also included and this does use the kit windscreen. Note the longer

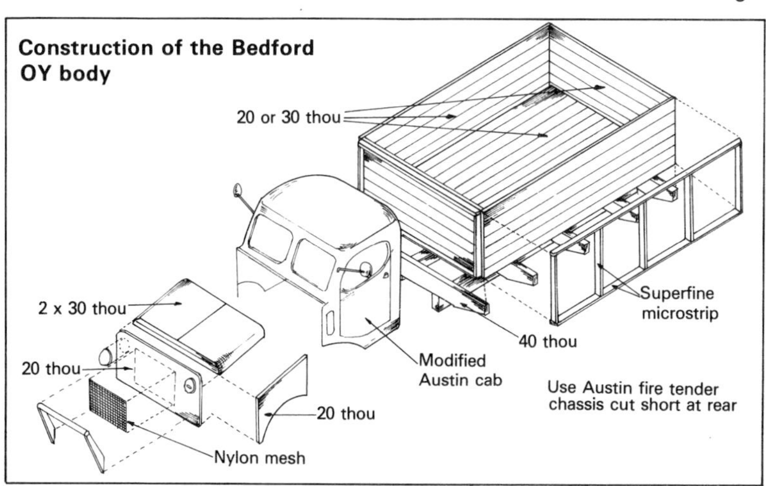

Construction of the Bedford OY body

wheelbase chassis of the C4. The C8 type van was also fitted to the C4 and note also that the water tanker as fitted to the Bedford MW could also be fitted to the Morris CS8 to give yet more permutations.

AEC Matador and gun kit

The Matador was used by the RAF in many guises and one of the simpler is a flat platform body tractor. Note this will need a new roof to replace that in the kit. Drawings for a wood body GS are also included.

I hope I have shown in this chapter a few of the simpler conversions possible from the various Airfix kits and that airfield dioramas can be enhanced with a few more of the many vehicles employed.

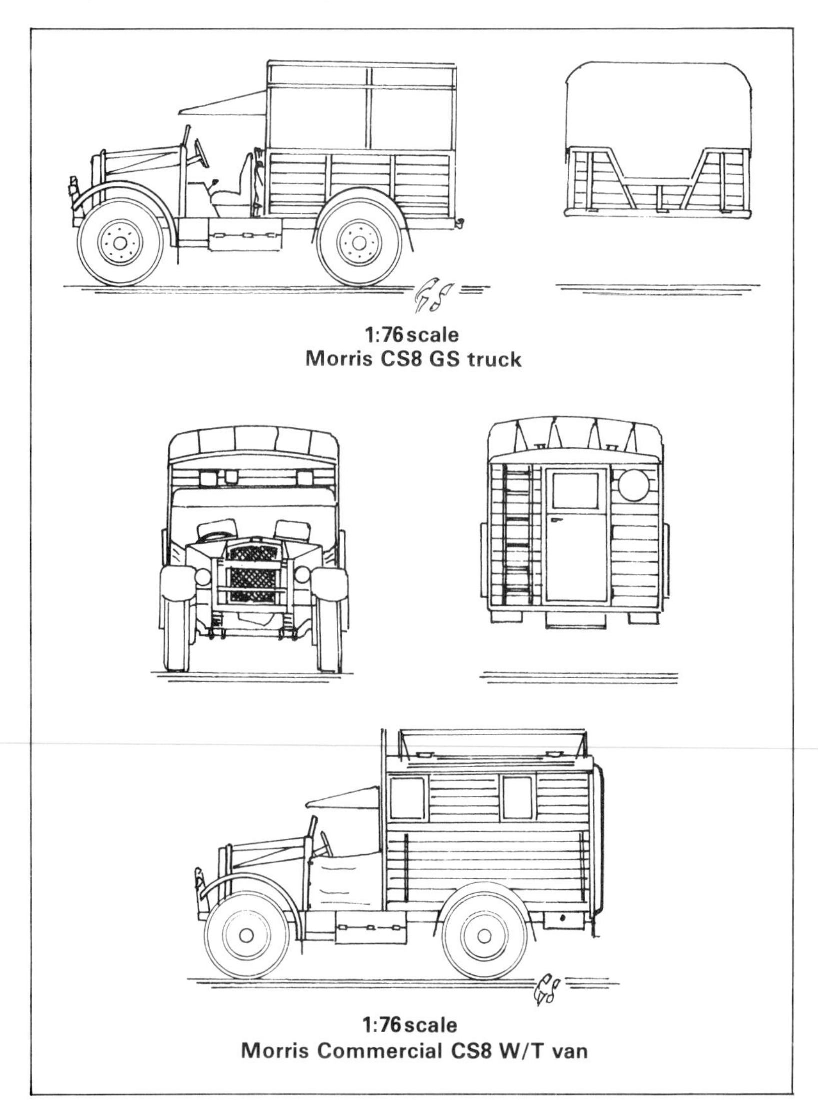

1:76 scale
Morris CS8 GS truck

1:76 scale
Morris Commercial CS8 W/T van

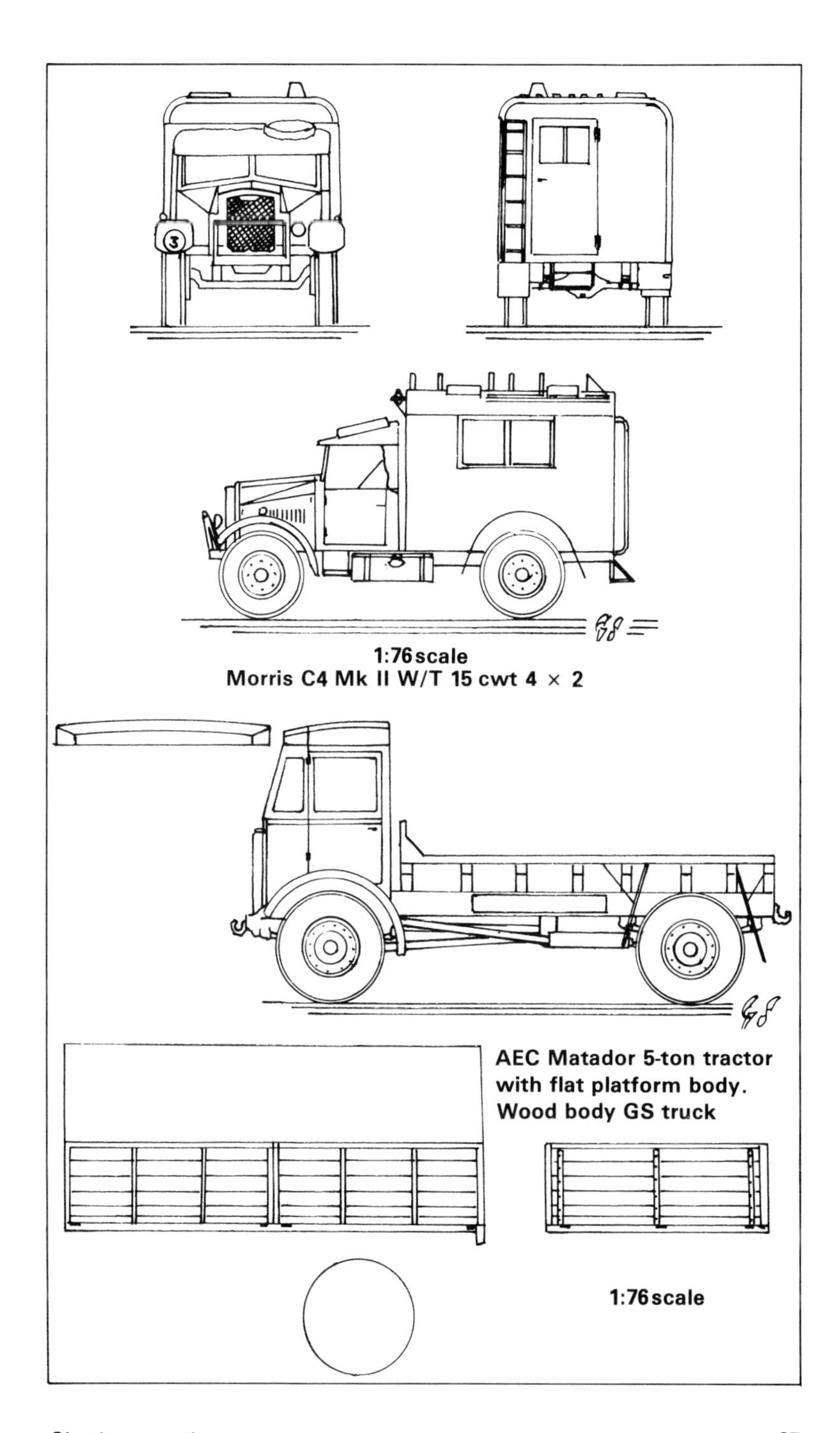

1:76 scale
Morris C4 Mk II W/T 15 cwt 4 × 2

AEC Matador 5-ton tractor with flat platform body. Wood body GS truck

1:76 scale

three

Workhorses of the early period

The RFC/RAF were early users of motor vehicles and in this chapter I hope to illustrate some of the various types that were used from World War 1 up to the outbreak of World War 2.

Clayton Shuttleworth tractor

Clayton Shuttleworth of Lincoln built Sopwith Camels and Handley Page 0/400 bombers during World War 1, both aircraft being subjects covered in the Airfix range. Clayton's were better known for fine agricultural engines, wagons and tractors and the subject of these drawings is a Clayton crawler tractor which was used by the War Department for, amongst other things, towing large aircraft. Among these was the 0/400.

A simple model of this tractor is not too difficult as it is basically a simple box for the engine with a channel section 'chassis'. Most of the running gear is hidden by the covers, the front idler can come from the Airfix PzKpfw IV as can

Clayton Shuttleworth tractor on display at Lincolnshire Agricultural Show. The rear view shows steering wheel, seat and rear axle.

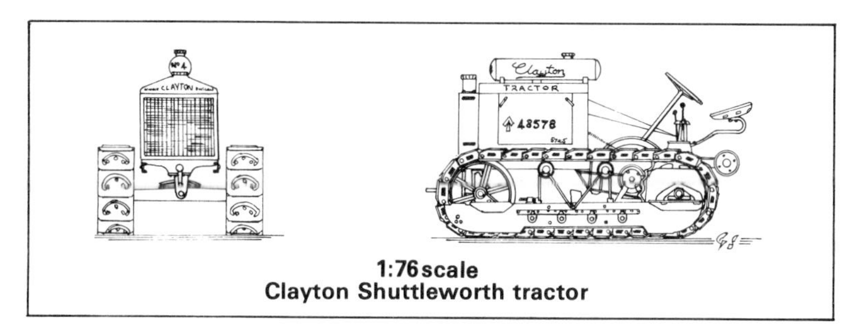

1:76 scale
Clayton Shuttleworth tractor

the roadwheels and top rollers. The track can be scratch-built based on strips of 10 thou plastic card embellished with stretched sprue tread. The cylindrical tank can be found in the Emergency set, while one of the gas cylinders and the steering wheel can come from one of the vehicle kits. The photographs were taken at Lincolnshire Agricultural Show and a tractor of this type is exhibited at the Lincoln Museum of Lincolnshire Life. Note the WD

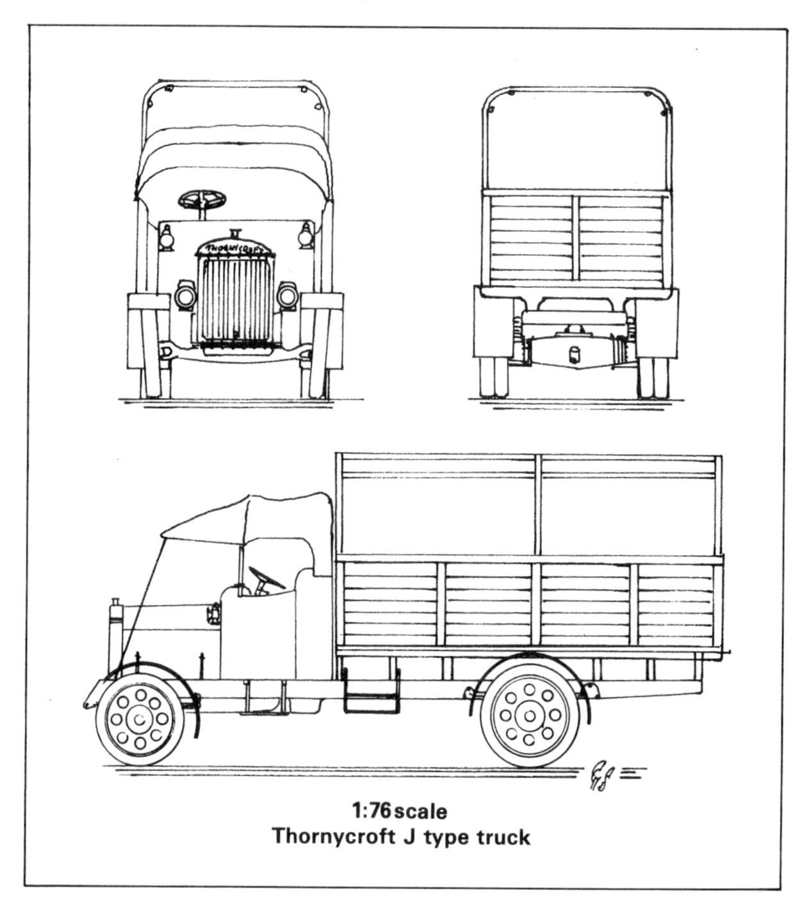

1:76 scale
Thornycroft J type truck

Albion Model BY3 6 × 4 typical of the Crossley, Leyland, Thornycroft, AEC and Karrier open-cabbed types on standardised WD chassis.

version had a longer tank and was fitted with a pulley winch to the rear axle power take-off.

Thornycroft J type

Models of early vehicles are easy subjects to scratch-build being based on simple chassis with little in the way of cab comforts or refinements. The Thornycroft J was a well used type and the GS truck drawn was one of the standard Thornycroft products. Wheels for this type of vehicle, solid tyred, disc wheels, are similar to those used on later

Believed to be an AEC Marshall, loaded with K5569 (P.H.T. Green Collection).

World War 2 and after, tanks. The Airfix kits of the Crusader, T-34, Panther, etc, can usually provide the raw materials for these and in this case, the Panther wheels can be used, drilling the typical 'holes' in the rim. Use twin convex wheels at the rear (with the bosses cut off) and add a rim of 10 thou plastic card and individual 'tyres' from Microstrip. An alternative is to mould rims of 20 thou plastic card with a centre disc of 20 thou cemented in place and Microstrip tyres.

Leyland Subsidy A type

Another famous 'RAF' type, the Leylands, of which both a fuel truck and a GS version are drawn, are essentially similar to Thornycroft. Wheels are again Airfix Panther tank but for the front ones use the convex type. The cylindrical tank can be made from wooden dowel or you may find a plastic

Front view of Leyland Subsidy.

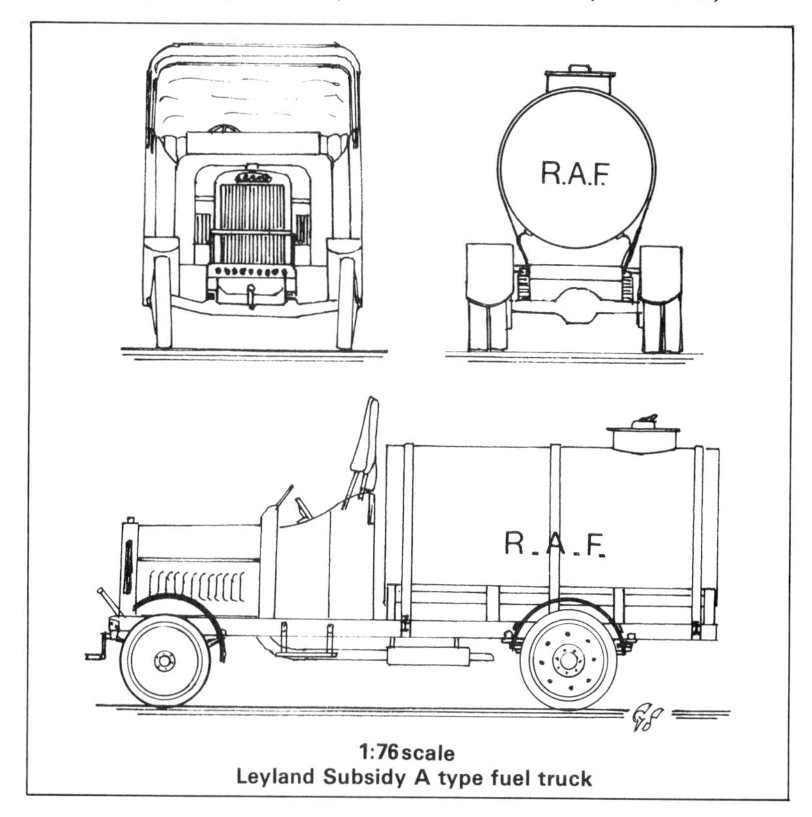

1:76 scale
Leyland Subsidy A type fuel truck

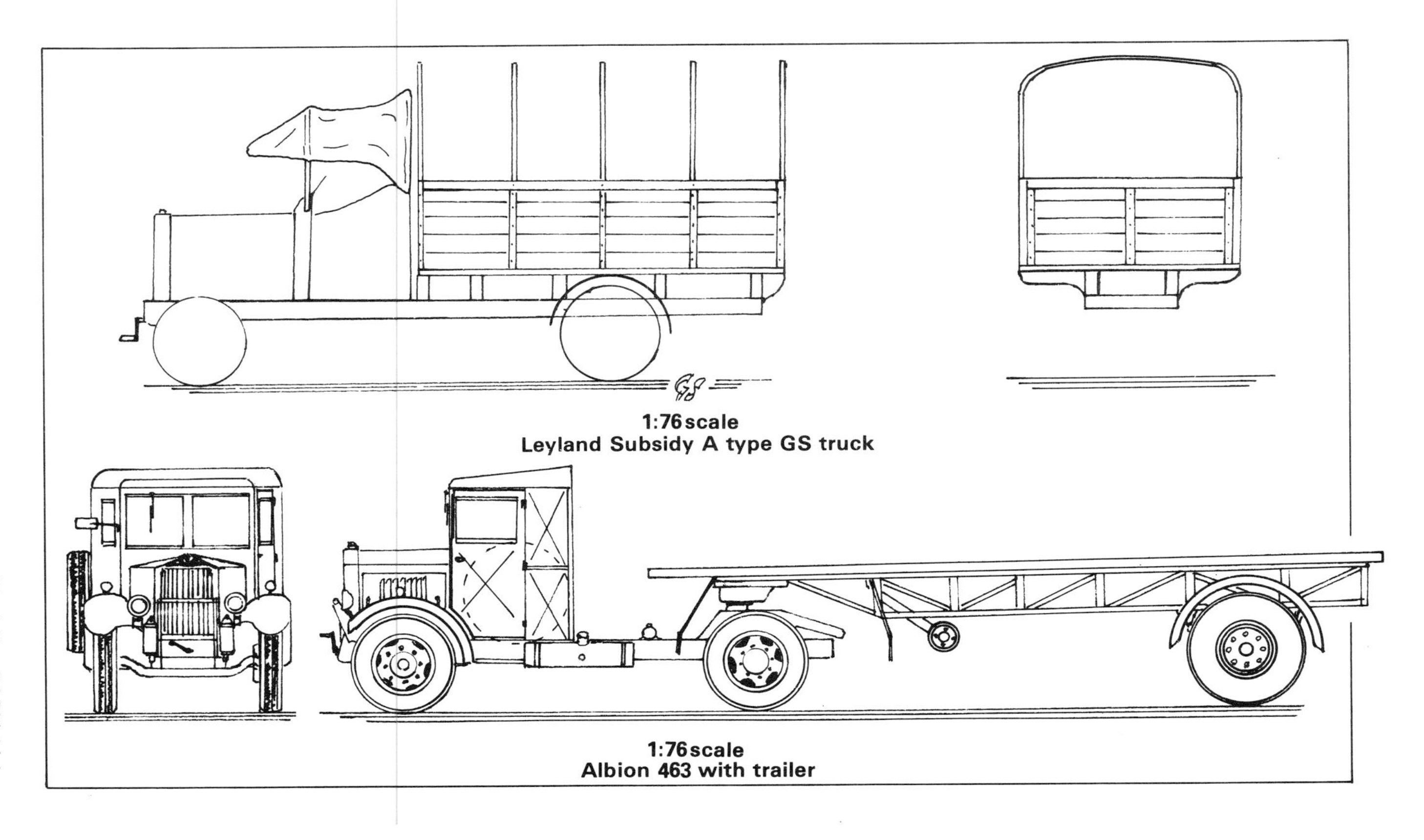

1:76 scale
Leyland Subsidy A type GS truck

1:76 scale
Albion 463 with trailer

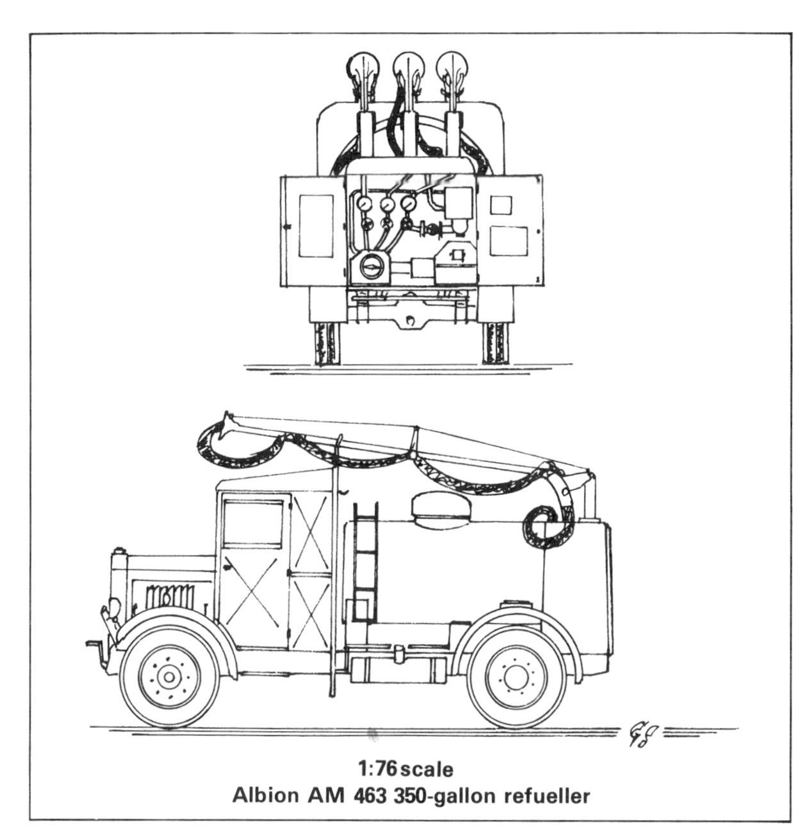

1:76 scale
Albion AM 463 350-gallon refueller

container, eg, a pill box or similar of correct size.

Albion AM 463

The Albion 350-gallon refueller was used in the 1930s and up to the early years of World War 2 until replaced by later types such as the Bedford QL in the Refuelling set. Parts of this kit can be used for the detail and either the Bedford wheels or those from the Austin (although a little small) can be utilised. The cab and bonnet are straightforward, the panel pressings in the sides, shown as 'X's, can be lightly ruled in from the reverse side to just raise a line. Practice on scrap first to get

Leyland Subsidy type GS truck.

Albion AM463 350 gallon refueller.

Albion refueller tanking up Hurricane BY-Q, which aircraft is the subject of the Airfix 1:24 scale kit (Neville Franklin Collection).

Albion AM463 tractor unit fitted with flat semi-trailer. Note the trailer could also be fitted to Commer, Bedford, etc.

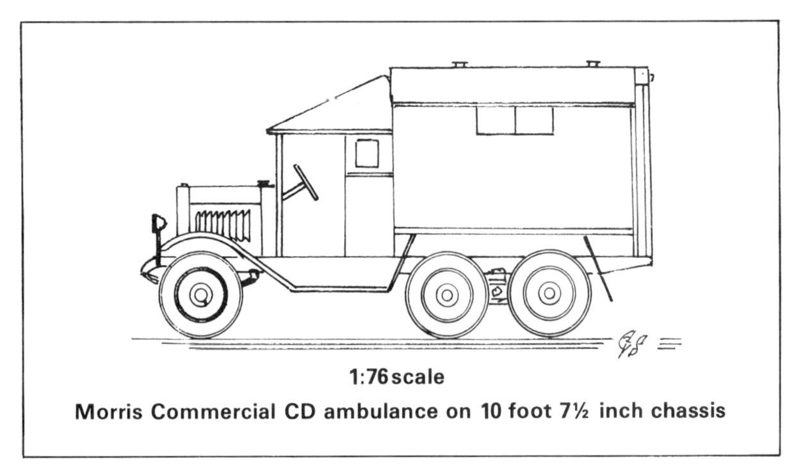

1:76 scale

Morris Commercial CD ambulance on 10 foot 7½ inch chassis

Morris Commercial vehicles somewhere in Arab regions. Unfortunately the natives clustered round spoil the view.

Ford T Hucks Starter about to be used on a Wappiti (Neville Franklin Collection).

Morris Commercial shown with sliding tilt forward over cab. This is a similar vehicle to that shown in the background of the above photograph.

the right pressure to use. Note the extended cab rear which comes below the chassis line.

This Albion chassis was also used as a semi-trailer tractor and the drawing shows one of these with a skeletal chassis semi-trailer.

Morris Commercial

The Morris Commercial CDF 30 cwt 6 × 4 was typical of the 1930s period, similar types being produced by Karrier, Thornycroft, Guy, Albion, Crossley, etc. The Bofors gun kit tractor supplies the essential wheels, axles, etc, and the chassis, cab and body are straightforward. Note the body is of 'well' type (shown dotted on the rear view) and the spare wheel is mounted on the offside with the fuel tank on the nearside behind the cab. The drawing of the ambulance represents the normal control version of this same chassis.

The truck/van version is on the 12-foot wheelbase chassis and the photographs of this loaded with a Bristol Fighter illustrates how the rear top section slides forward over the cab/bonnet. Note the top corners of the tilt are 'solid' as is the front quarter of the body. The rear three-quarters of the sides are covered with canvas.

Ford T

The Ford T Hucks Starter saw service between the wars when engines were getting a bit much to swing by hand and

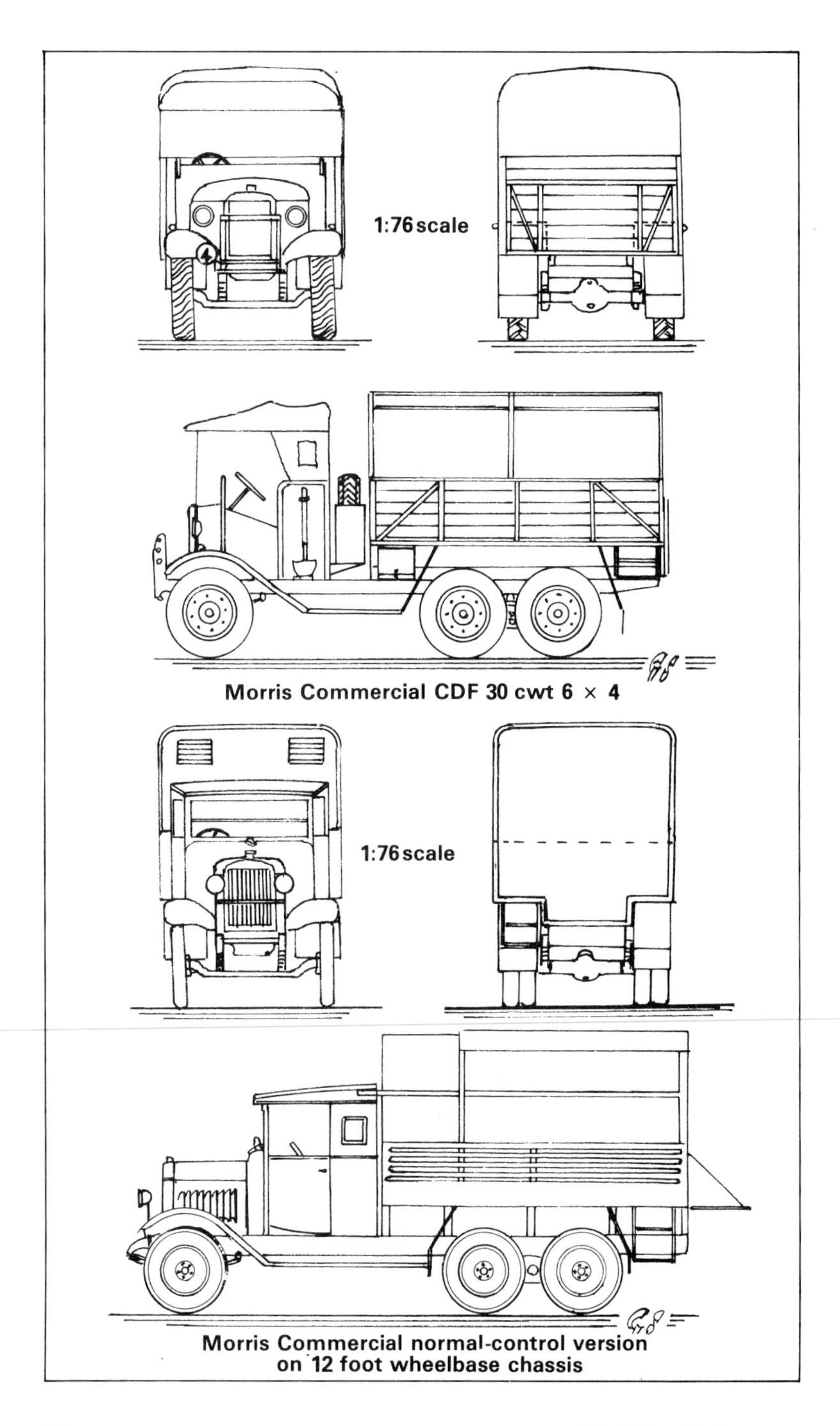

Morris Commercial CDF 30 cwt 6 × 4

Morris Commercial normal-control version on 12 foot wheelbase chassis

Morris Commercial GS truck with full width windscreen typical of C4 types (Terry Gander).

Morris Commercial CS8 with aero screens.

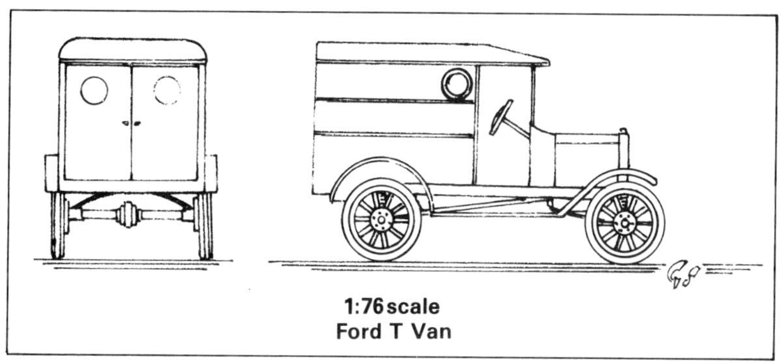

1:76 scale
Ford T Van

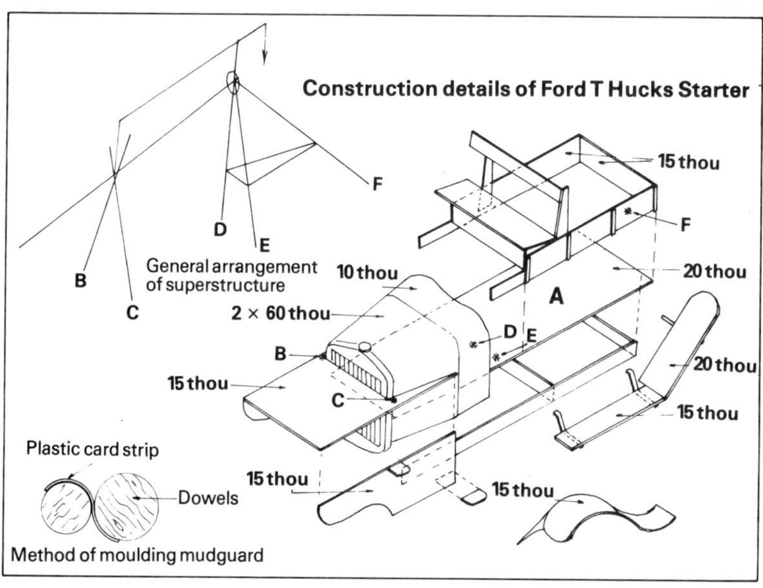

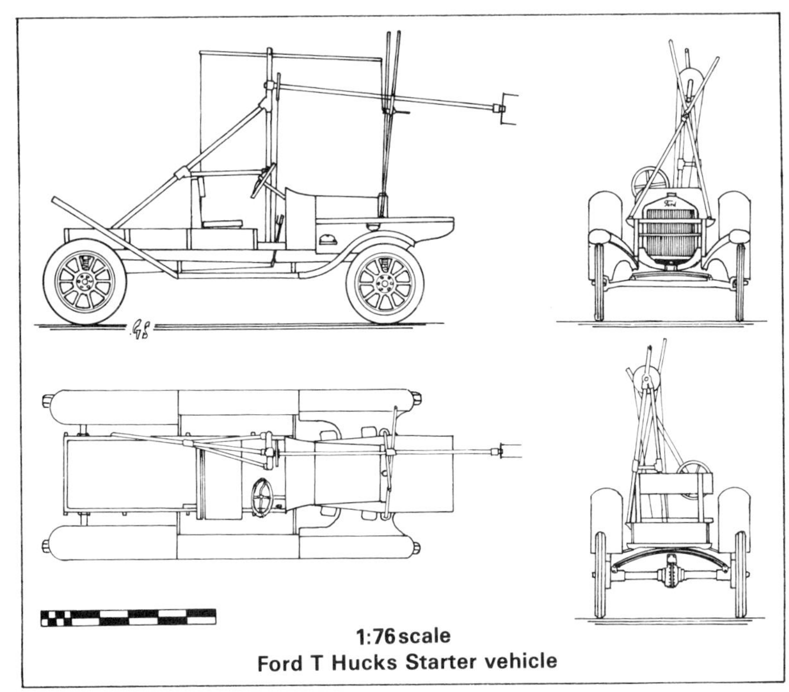

1:76 scale
Ford T Hucks Starter vehicle

before the advent of the other starting devices. The wheels on this vehicle, although tricky, could be scratch-built from Microstrip and plastic rod. Construction of the rest of the model should be clear from the sketch.

The van version is typical of the type of light delivery truck used by the RAF late in World War 1 and just after this period.

Trojan 10 hp van

A neat little model can be made from the simple Trojan 5 cwt van, as the

Two Rolls-Royce armoured cars shown with attendant Morris Commercial 6 × 4 (Neville Franklin Collection).

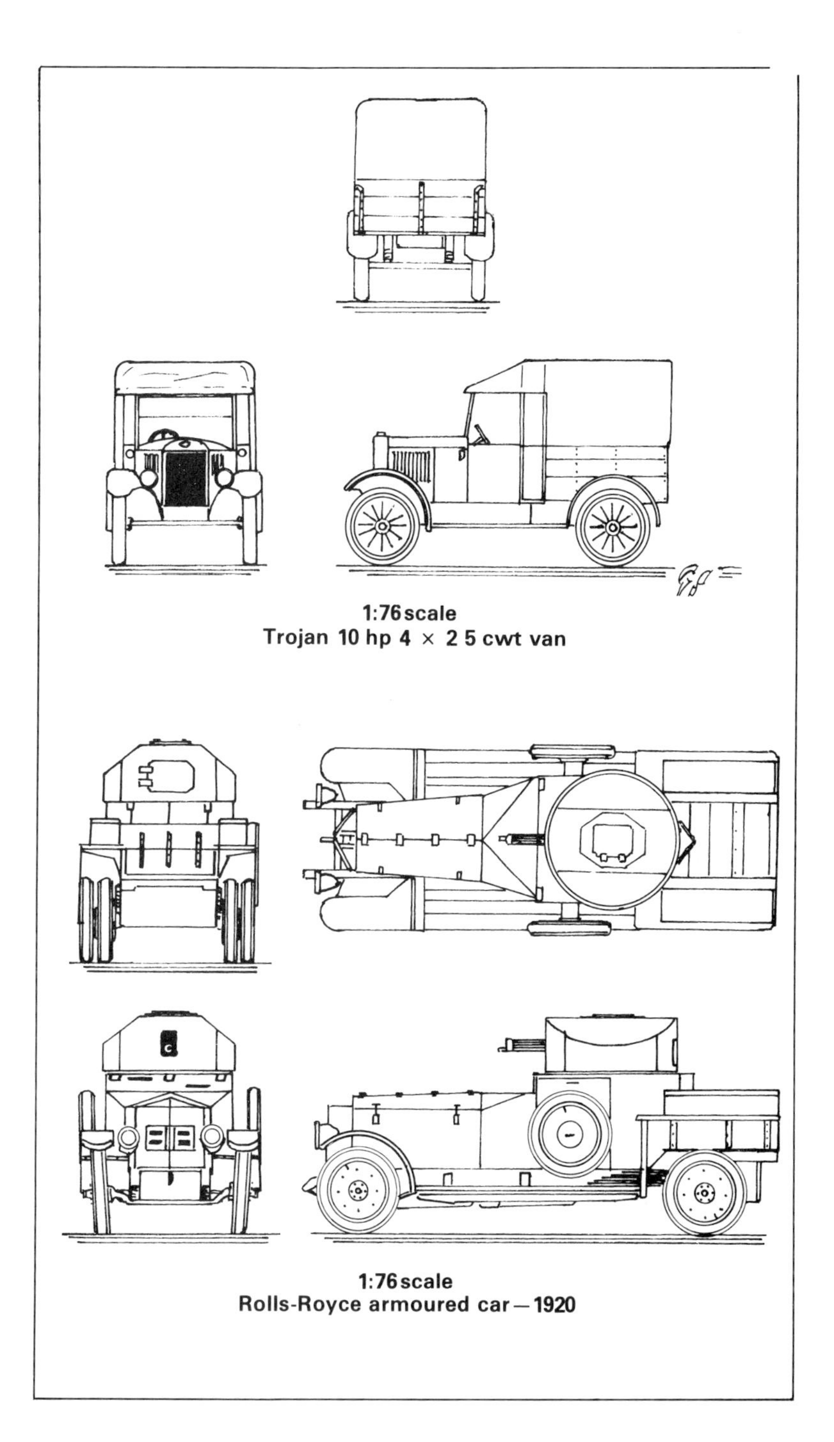

1:76 scale
Trojan 10 hp 4 × 2 5 cwt van

1:76 scale
Rolls-Royce armoured car — 1920

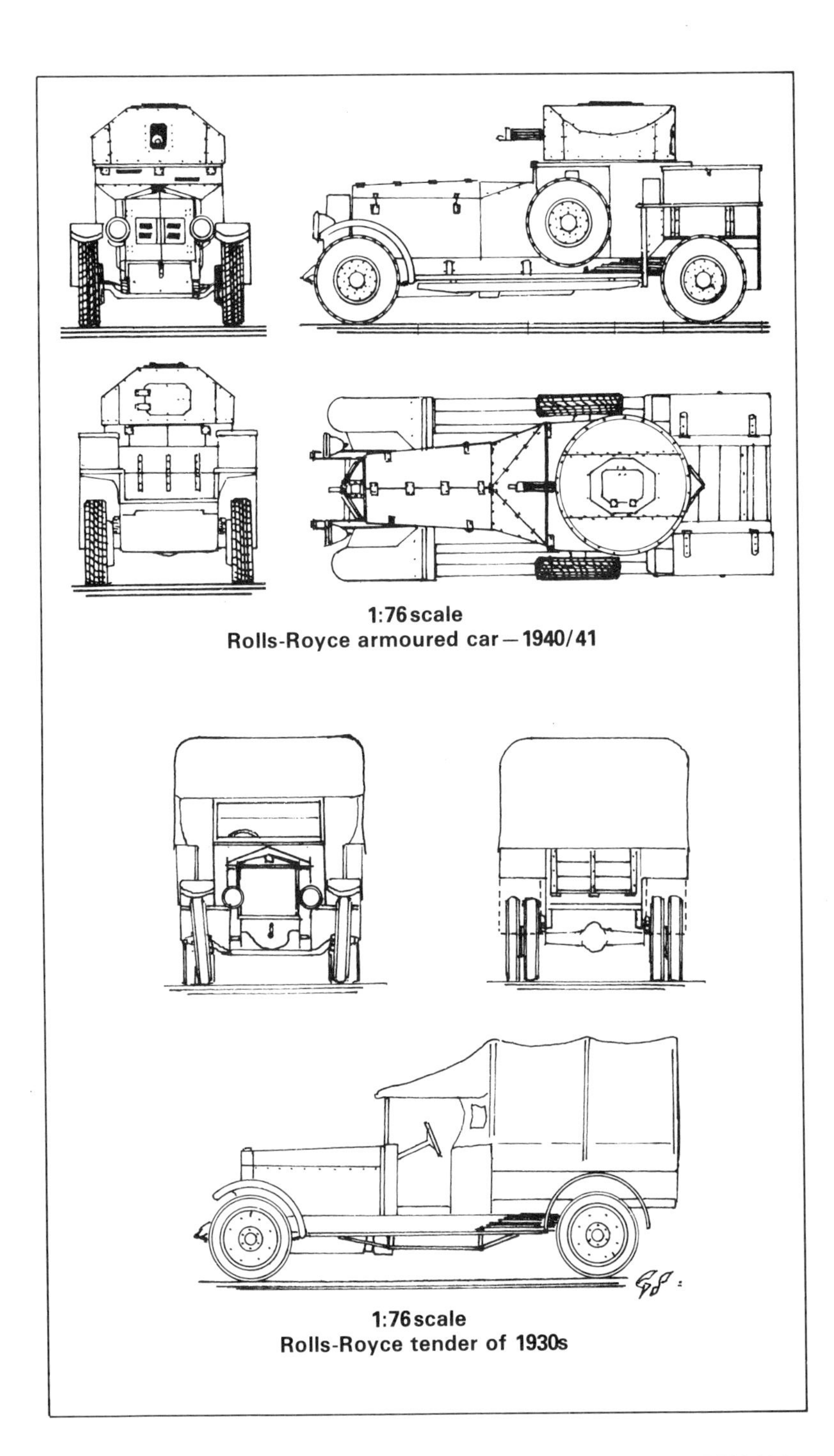

1:76 scale
Rolls-Royce armoured car – 1940/41

1:76 scale
Rolls-Royce tender of 1930s

Rolls-Royce armoured car HMAC Shark.

wheels were of disc type (you could ignore the cast strengthening webs) and are made from plastic card discs with a rim of 10 thou Microstrip and a tyre of 20 thou Microstrip, slightly rounded off at the edges.

Rolls-Royce

The Rolls-Royce armoured cars (the RFC, RNAS and RAF were great users of armoured cars for airfield defence and aquisition) were also typical of the period between the wars. Drawings are included for the 1920 pattern armoured car and a later 1940/41 version fitted with sand tyres. This was described in more detail in *Airfix Guide 21—Modelling Armoured Cars*. Bedford wheels from the Recovery set were used for this and I suggested that for the 1920 pattern Airfix Hawker Demon or similar wheels could be used for the front pair with Crusader tank roadwheels or similar for the twin rears. The tender also based on this chassis is another vehicle typical of the period.

Crossley 4 × 2 four-seater car

The Crossley was the standard RFC/ RAF squadron runabout from World

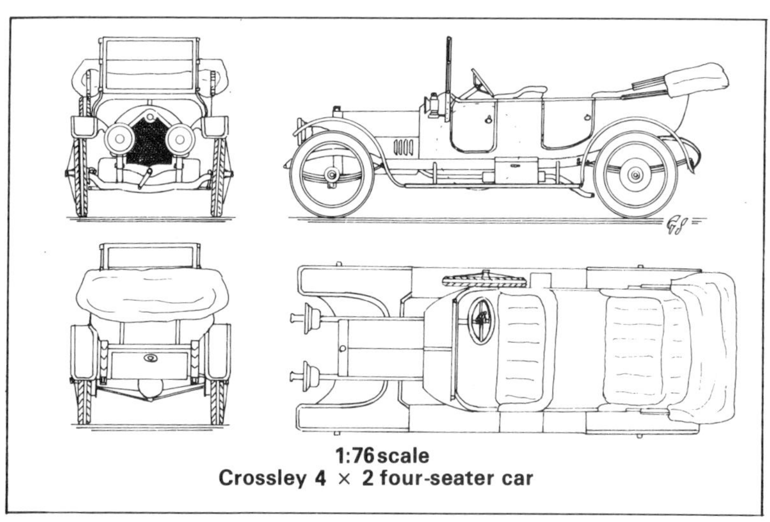

1:76 scale
Crossley 4 × 2 four-seater car

Rear view of Crossley showing fuel tank and rear spring detail.

Crossley tourer as preserved at Shuttleworth.

War 1 to about 1929 30—what a delightful subject it would make for a kit in 1:32 scale! Visitors to the Shuttleworth Trust will have seen their Crossley still earning its keep giving joy-rides and the drawings were prepared from measurements of this particular car. My thanks to Wing Commander T.E. Guttery, MBE, for his permission to examine their car.

A model to join your collection seems to present some problems in this small scale but, of course, as it is so small it is not essential to add every bit of detail. The delicate-appearing spoked wheels are number one and there are several ways these can be made. I suggest the tyres can be cut as slices from a plastic tube, say an old ballpoint pen case, and filed to section. An alternative is to try the spares department of a tractor dealer and get him to sort out some of the little plastic/rubber hydraulic 'O' ring seals used in the hydraulic control valves. I have some from the Ford range of tractors that are perfect for the job. Next make up the rims from Microstrip to go inside the tyres. Inside these fit a disc of clear plastic on to which you can score some spokes which can be accented by rubbing in Indian Ink. Cement a hub shaped from sprue into

Detail of front of Crossley.

the centre of the disc and if you are a masochist add outside spokes from stretched sprue. Note there are only brake drums to the rear wheels. Some models were fitted with twin tyred rims at the rear as shown on the photographs of the early Crossley tender.

Construction is now based on two chassis frames cut from 40 thou plastic card cemented underneath a 'floor' to the body as was done for the Ford T. The bonnet, from 20 thou with a 60 thou plastic card radiator, the scuttle carved and filed from laminations of plastic card, and the body from 30 thou plastic card, are built up to the floor. Mudguards are moulded round dowel and the running boards are formed from 15 thou plastic card with the tool box fitted on assembly—this will help support the running boards/mudguards. On the offside a spare wheel protrudes through the running board with a small box behind this. Note there is no driver's door, it is a three-door car. Note the rear

Rear wheel detail of Crossley. Note oval fuel tank and three-quarter eliptic rear springs.

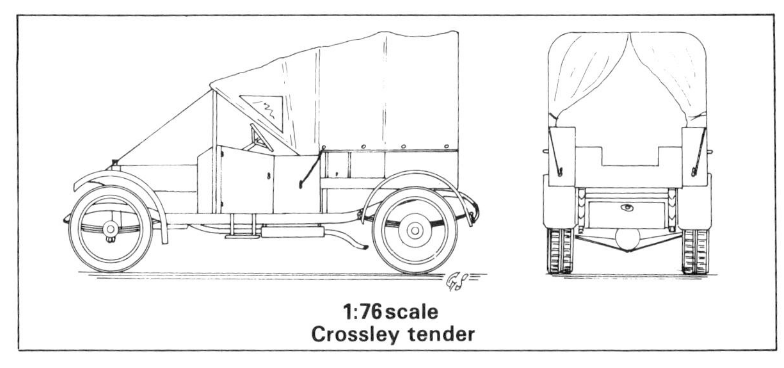

1:76 scale
Crossley tender

Crossley tender with twin tyred rear wheels.

springs are three-quarter eliptic and the fronts half-eliptic. The rear fuel tank between the springs is of oval section.

Crossley tender

The Crossley chassis was used as a basis for tenders, 15 cwt trucks, ambulances, etc, some on an 11 foot 3 inch wheelbase chassis. The drawing is for a tender on the same chassis as the tourer car and is obviously a lot simpler to make. A preserved example can be seen at the Royal Air Force Museum at Hendon. The chassis, bonnet, wheels and twin tyred rears are all as for the car but for the scuttle, which is much simpler than the car, so the model is like any other pick-up or small lorry.

And that is just a few of the many interesting and varied vehicles used by the RAF from World War 1 to the outbreak of World War 2. Some of these soldiered on well into World War 2, some came back into civilian use and a very few are still preserved, some even in running order. One particular Leyland Subsidy type which served in World War 1 was among those re-purchased by Leylands, reconditioned and then re-sold with a two-year guarantee. It was bought by Chivers and Son Ltd of Cambridge in 1919, fitted with a box-type body and used for delivery work until 1934 when it was retired from general work in their factory at Histon. It was then converted into a water carrier as part of the factory's fire brigade in World War 2, subsequently working on the Chivers Farms until 1959 when it was completely restored and later presented to the Historic Commercial Vehicle Club. I wonder if any vehicles coming from Leyland today will still be going in the year 2035?

four

World War 2 trucks, cars and bodies

World War 2 saw a tremendous increase in the numbers and types of vehicles used by all the armed forces and the RAF, with its own special requirements, used a vast range of chassis and body types. In this chapter we will consider a few of these to try to give a typical cross-section.

Many small pick-up trucks and vans were to be seen scuttling around airfields on communications, haulage and crew transport jobs and no fighter station was complete without its Austin, Morris, Hillman or Standard into which the crews would cram to be taken to their aircraft.

Light trucks

These types are essentially similar and I have included drawings of the Standard 12, Austin G/YG and Morris M light utilities with the Standard 14 hp

Standard 12 light utility (Terry Gander).

Hillman 10 hp light utility (Terry Gander).

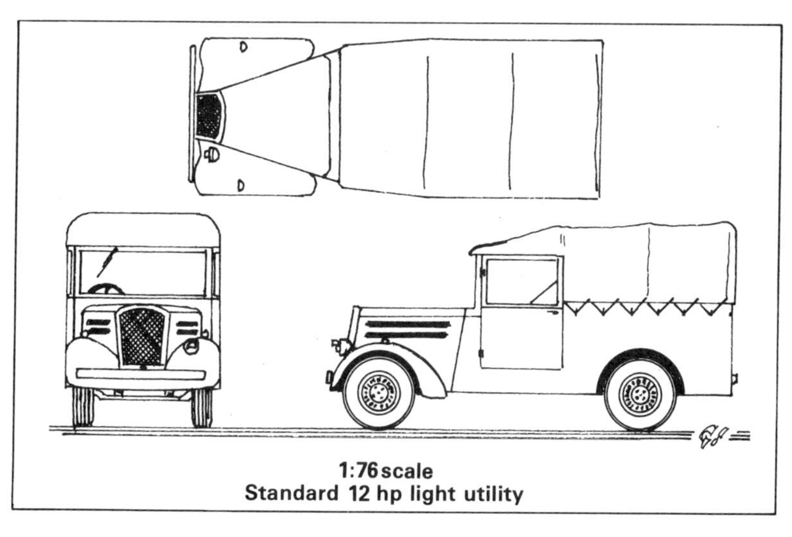

1:76 scale
Standard 12 hp light utility

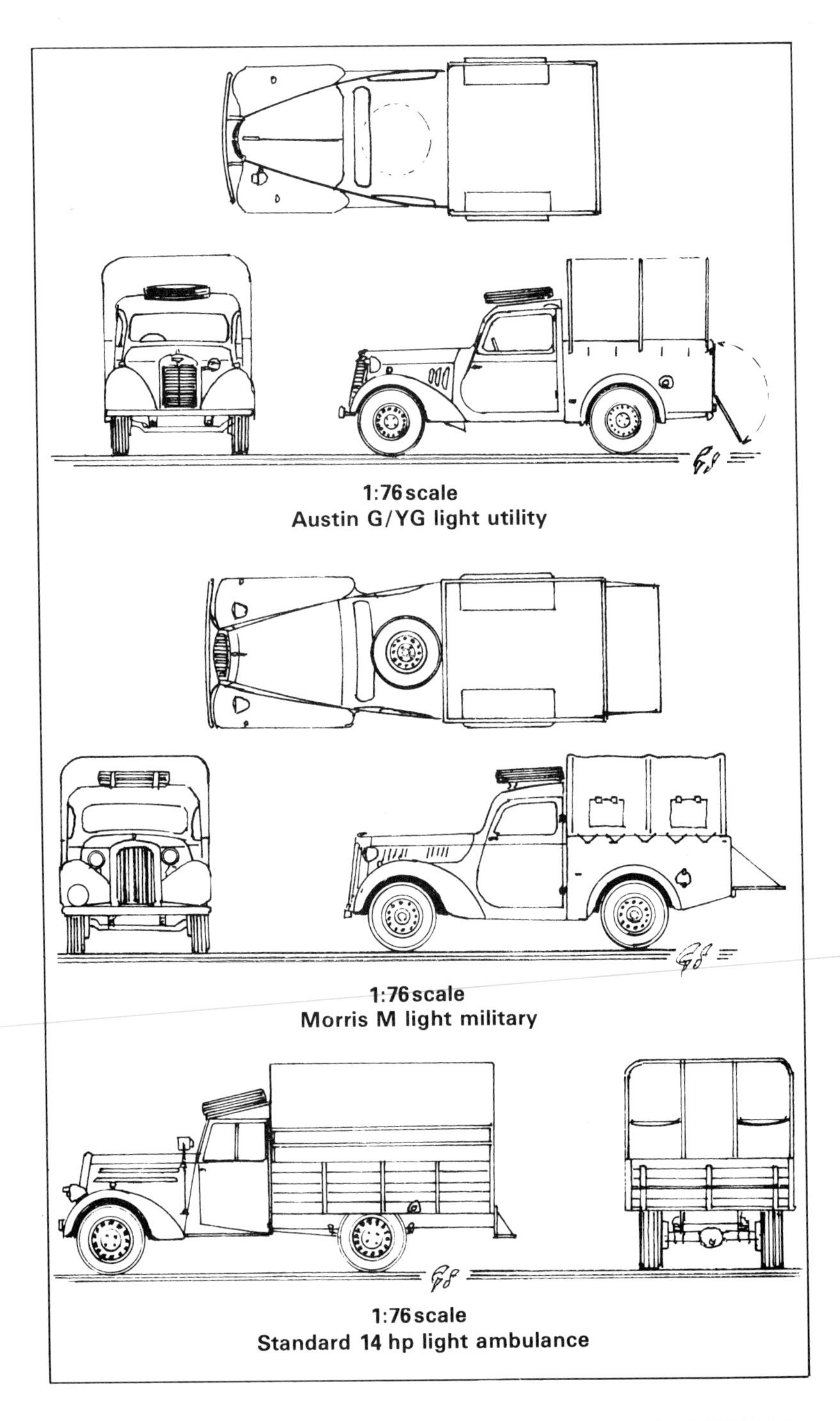

1:76 scale
Austin G/YG light utility

1:76 scale
Morris M light military

1:76 scale
Standard 14 hp light ambulance

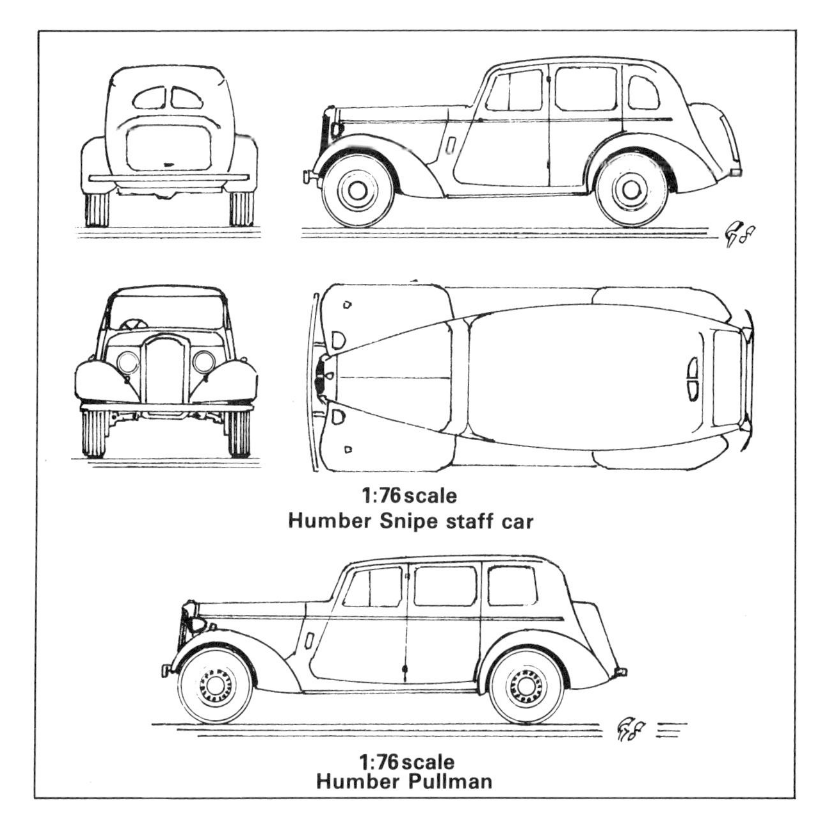

1:76 scale
Humber Snipe staff car

1:76 scale
Humber Pullman

as an example of the light ambulances used on and around home airfields.

Wheels suitable for these small vehicles can be found in the Airfix German Reconnaissance set, the Volkswagen or from the Jeep in the Buffalo Amphibian set. I don't think the incorrect wheel centre detail is too important in this scale and the knobbly tread of the Jeep is quite acceptable as they were fitted with a 'town and country' type of tyre. Axles need be nothing more elaborate than plastic rod or cocktail sticks and the bodies and cab are quite simple to fabricate, provided that thick enough plastic card is chosen to enable the rounded corners and curves to be filed to shape. The front mudguards may cause problems and I would suggest moulding round a wooden former or, if your technique is not yet up to that, they can easily be shaped from Plasticine and stuck in place to the bonnet sides. A further simple method is to build up the shape with Plastic Padding or body putty and then file to shape when dry.

Humber staff cars

'Top Brass' usually travelled in more style and the Humber Snipe and the larger wheelbase Humber Pullman were favourites. Construction is a little more complicated than the trucks and my method is to build up the basic box shape from plastic card, leaving window apertures, of course, and then building up the contours with body putty, finally filing and sanding to shape. Land-Rover wheels from the Bristol Bloodhound missile kit can be utilised although they will have to be reduced slightly in overall diameter. Wheels from old toys, especially the early Matchbox ones, could be a useful alternative.

Preserved Humber Snipe-type staff car (Terry Gander).

Standard Beaverette

As representative of the many small armoured cars used for airfield defence, the Standard Beaverette Mk III drawing is included. One of the photographs shows Mk I and Mk III cut-down Beaverettes in use in 1946 as Slingsby Cadet glider tugs at Coleby Grange. Among the types of armoured car used by the RAF were: GMC Otter, Marmon Herrington, AEC, Morris LAC, Humber LRC, Humber Mks II and III and Staghound. Use was also made of Universal Carriers and various tanks were also RAF manned—but that is

A use could still be found for Standard Beaverettes as glider recovery vehicles. Slingsby T7 Cadet gliders at Coleby Grange in 1946 (P.H.T. Green Collection).

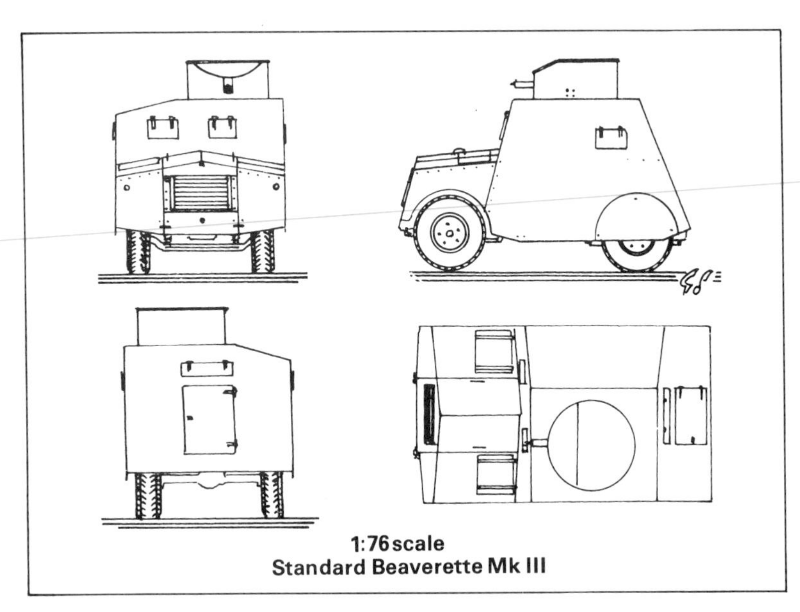

1:76 scale
Standard Beaverette Mk III

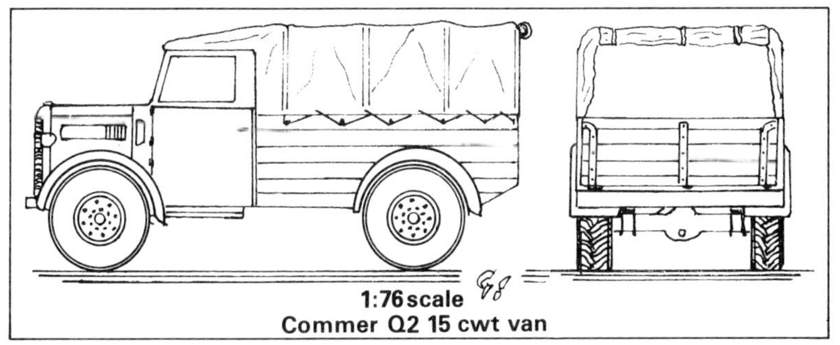
1:76 scale
Commer Q2 15 cwt van

really another story outside the capacity of this book.

Commer Q2

The Commer Q2 15 cwt van was strictly an RAF type, the metal body being built integral with the cab. A very simple model for which the Austin K6 wheels can be used. Note the radiator pattern and bonnet is as the drawing of the Q15 and that the cab in plan view widens out from the engine bulkhead to the full width of the body.

Commer Q15

A truck version of the Q2, the Q15, can be produced using wheels from the Bedford tractor unit in the Recovery set.

Commer Q2 tractor unit

This tractor unit makes a very acceptable alternative to the Bedford for use with the Airfix Queen Mary semi-trailer. Study of the plans will show that the basic shape is simple with only rounded corners to the back of the cab. This tractor unit can also be used with the flat semi-trailer shown on the drawing of the Albion AM463. Wheels again are from the Austin K6 or the Bedford QL.

Ford WOT 3 workshop

Typical of the smaller, boxy workshop trucks used by the RAF is the Ford WOT 3 which can also be made in GS truck form. The ever useful Emergency

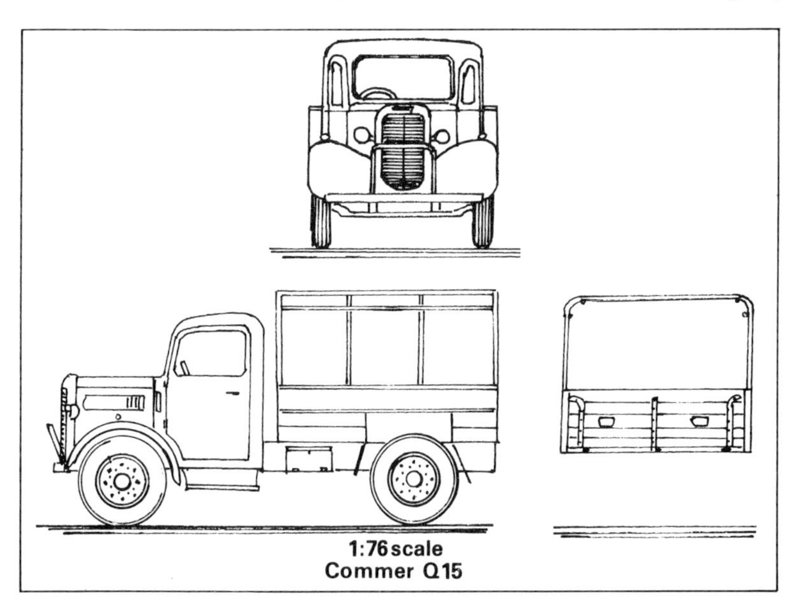
1:76 scale
Commer Q15

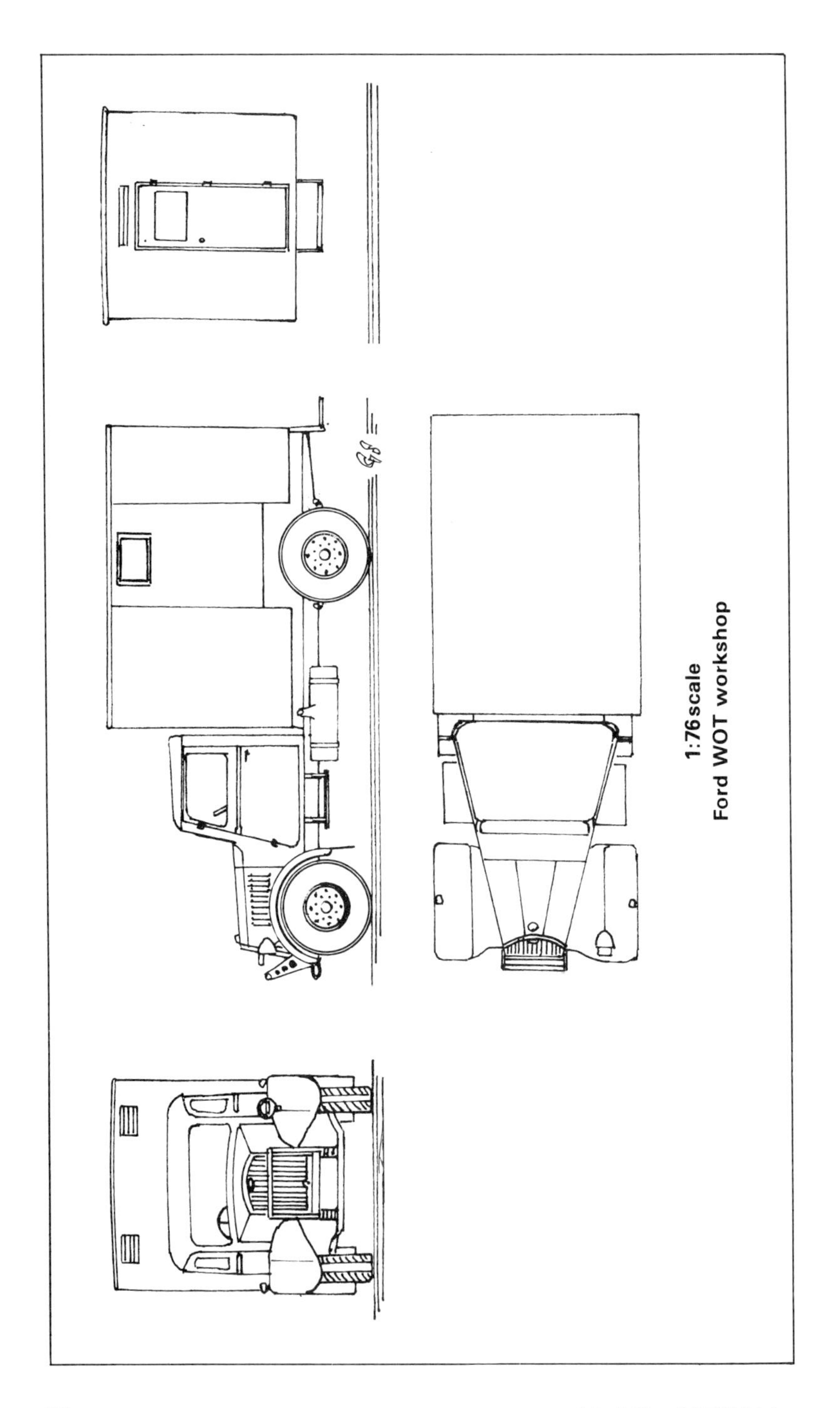

1:76 scale
Ford WOT workshop

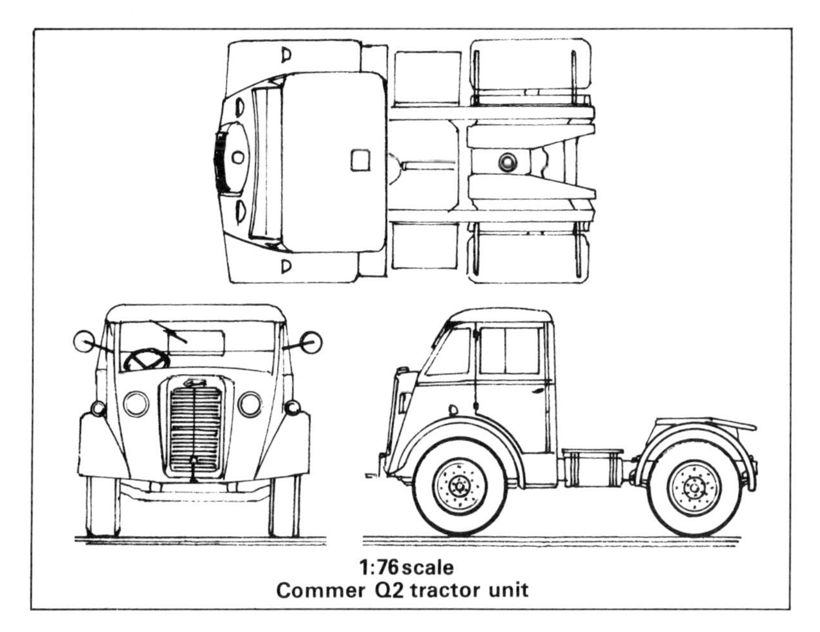
1:76 scale
Commer Q2 tractor unit

set can again be robbed for the wheels, axles and springs. The bonnet and cab sides are cut out in one piece using 20 thou plastic card building to a floor of 30 thou plastic card which is cut to fit inside the side pieces. The cab roof and bonnet top are from 60 thou plastic card, carved and filed to shape. The chassis frame can also be made from 60 thou and I suggest at least 30 thou for the body sides and ends with additional strengthening inside in the form of bulkheads.

The 30 cwt GS truck version has a spare wheel mounted behind the cab to the offside, the gap between cab and body being 5 mm. The body is 37 mm long by 28 mm wide with sides 9 mm high. Note on both models the fuel tanks, one either side, are of cylindrical section.

Ford WOT 6 × 4 3-ton dropside GS truck

Another early World War 2 type which, in fact, soldiered on for many years in different body styles, the

Fordson Sussex—a similar type of balloon winch vehicle to the Ford described (Neville Franklin Collection).

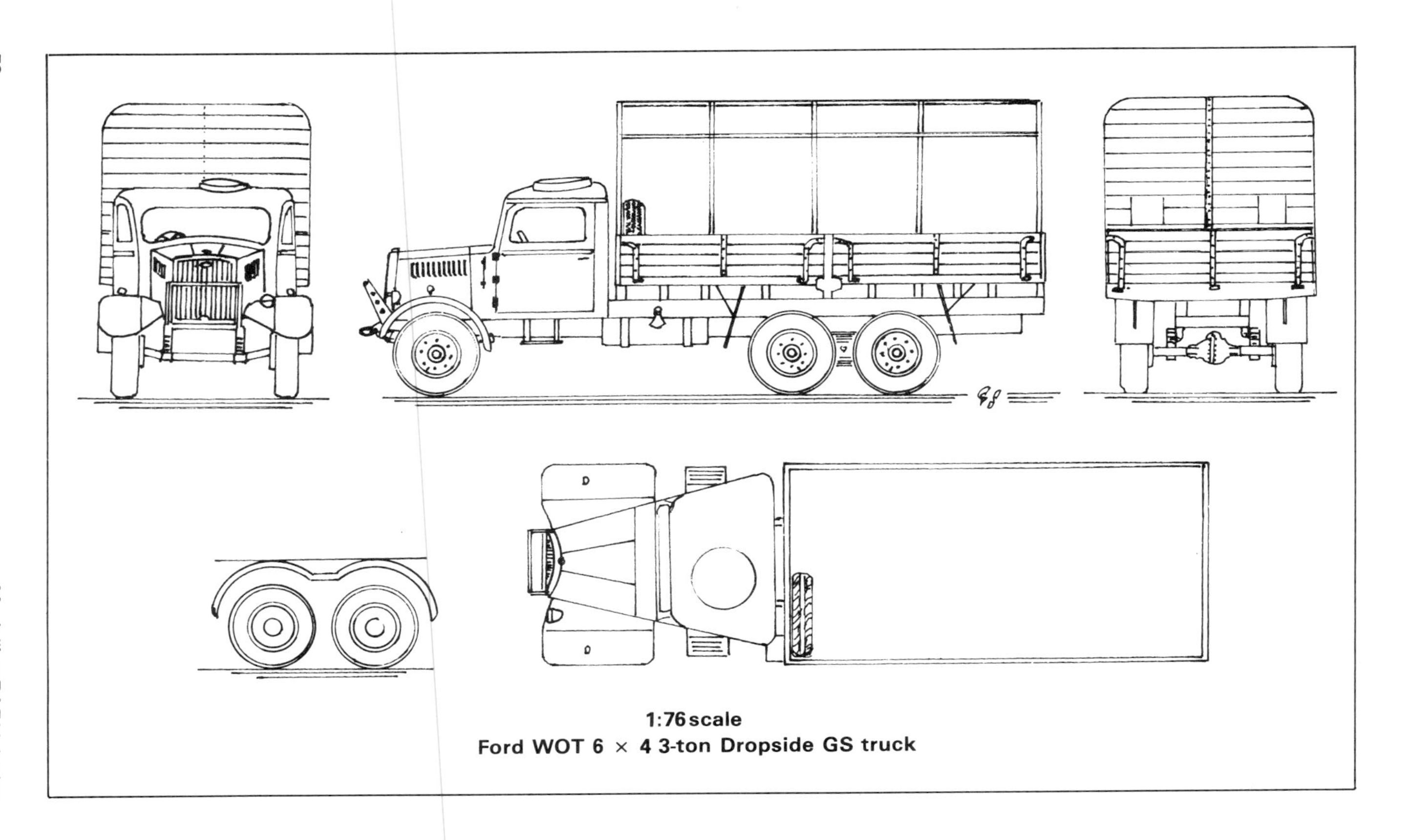

1:76 scale
Ford WOT 6 × 4 3-ton Dropside GS truck

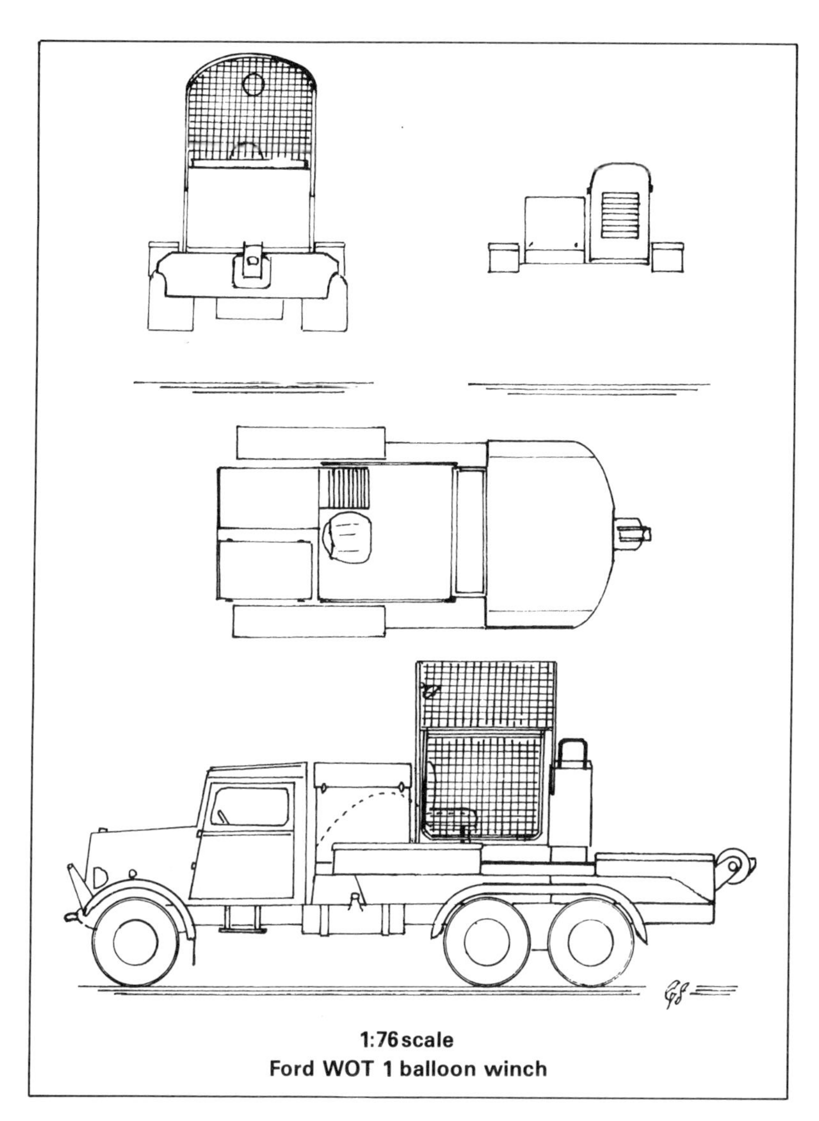

1:76 scale
Ford WOT 1 balloon winch

WOT 1 is drawn in dropside GS truck form. It was also fitted with the Cole Mk VII crane and crewbus (see drawings of Austin K6) and as generator and office trucks, etc. The cab is as the WOT 3 but sometimes fitted with a hip ring. Wheels from the Bofors gun tractor, with some of the knobblyness filed away, could be used, and often the rears were fitted with domed hub caps. This was especially so on the balloon winch version, the subject of the second WOT 1 drawing. Construction here is basically as already discussed and all the winch fittings can be based on a platform of 20 thou plastic card. Note the heavy cast rear end which can be built up from laminations of plastic card. The winch and winch engine covers, storage boxes and control console are simple basic box shapes. Fit the operator's seat and paint

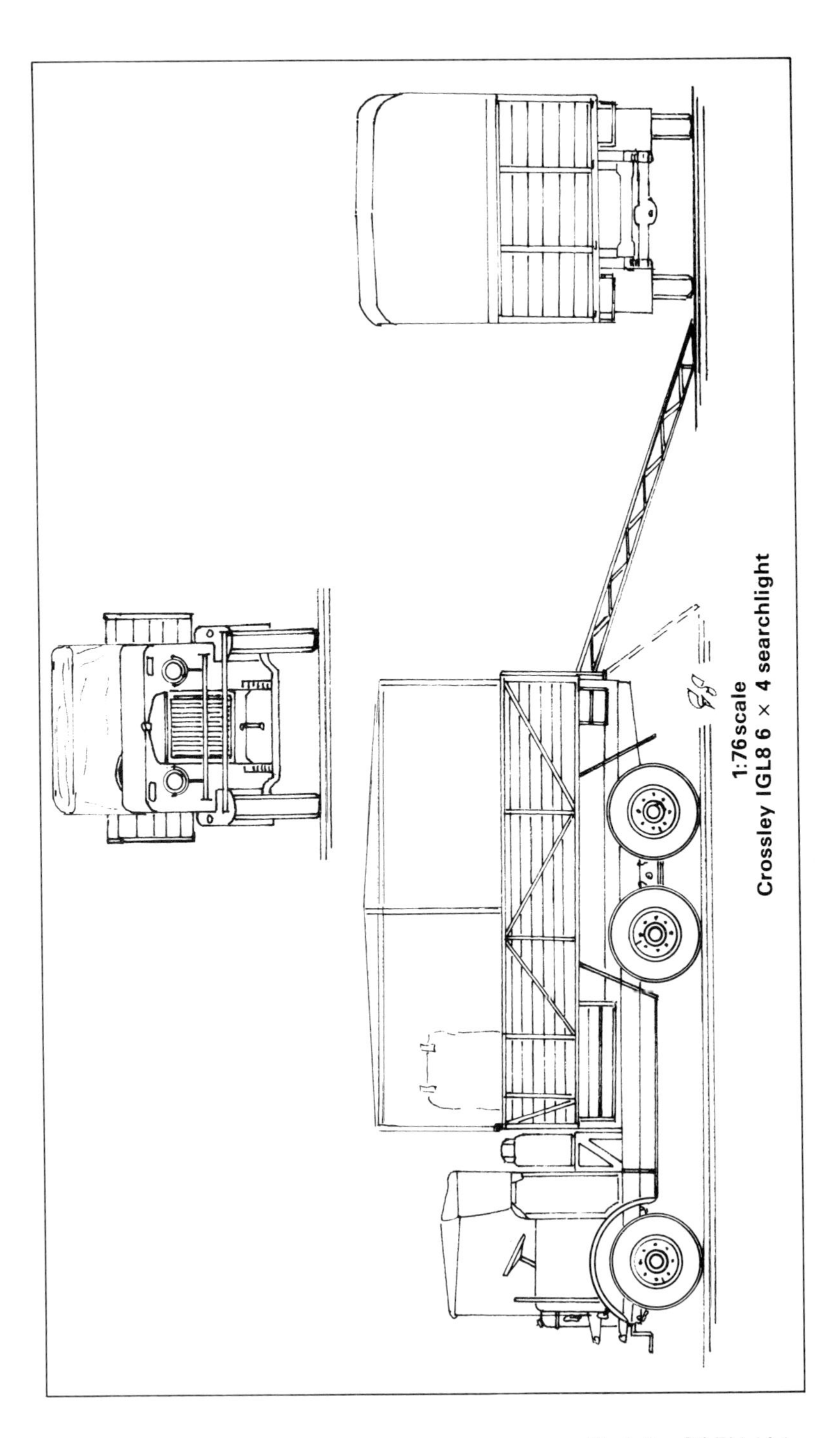
1:76 scale
Crossley IGL8 6 × 4 searchlight

Fordson WOT 1 chassis fitted with balloon winch (Neville Franklin Collection).

all the interior before fitting the cage of nylon mesh over a plastic rod frame.

Balloon

The winch vehicle is little use without a balloon so a drawing for this is included to 1:76 scale. If you have access to a lathe this could be turned up from soft wood and either finished in wood or used as a former to mould a shell from plastic card. As the size is not too important, a simpler method for the 'kitchen table' modeller is to take an ordinary 'festive' balloon and blow it up to as near the required shape and size as possible. A shell can now be built up on this using papier mâché, layers of thin tissue or newspaper soaked in paste. When dry the balloon could be deflated and the fins and extras added.

Plasticine can be used as a former for papier mâché fins. Several coats of clear varnish and sanding down should give a good basic shape and if cotton is used to define the panels of the envelope while the varnish is still tacky this will add the

Fordson with balloon fitted with parachutist training gondola. Vehicle on extreme left appears to be a Thornycroft ZS/TC4.

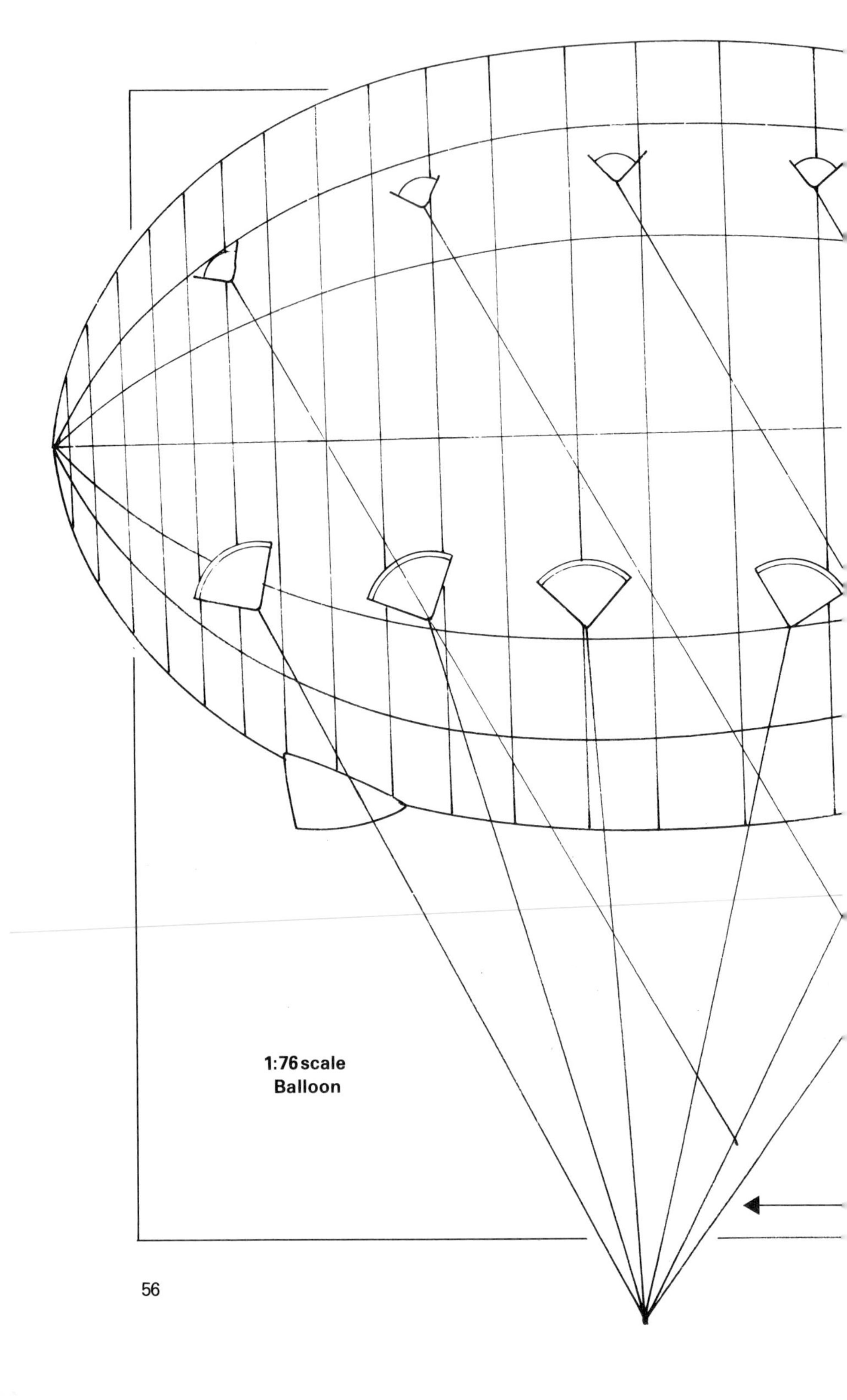
1:76 scale
Balloon

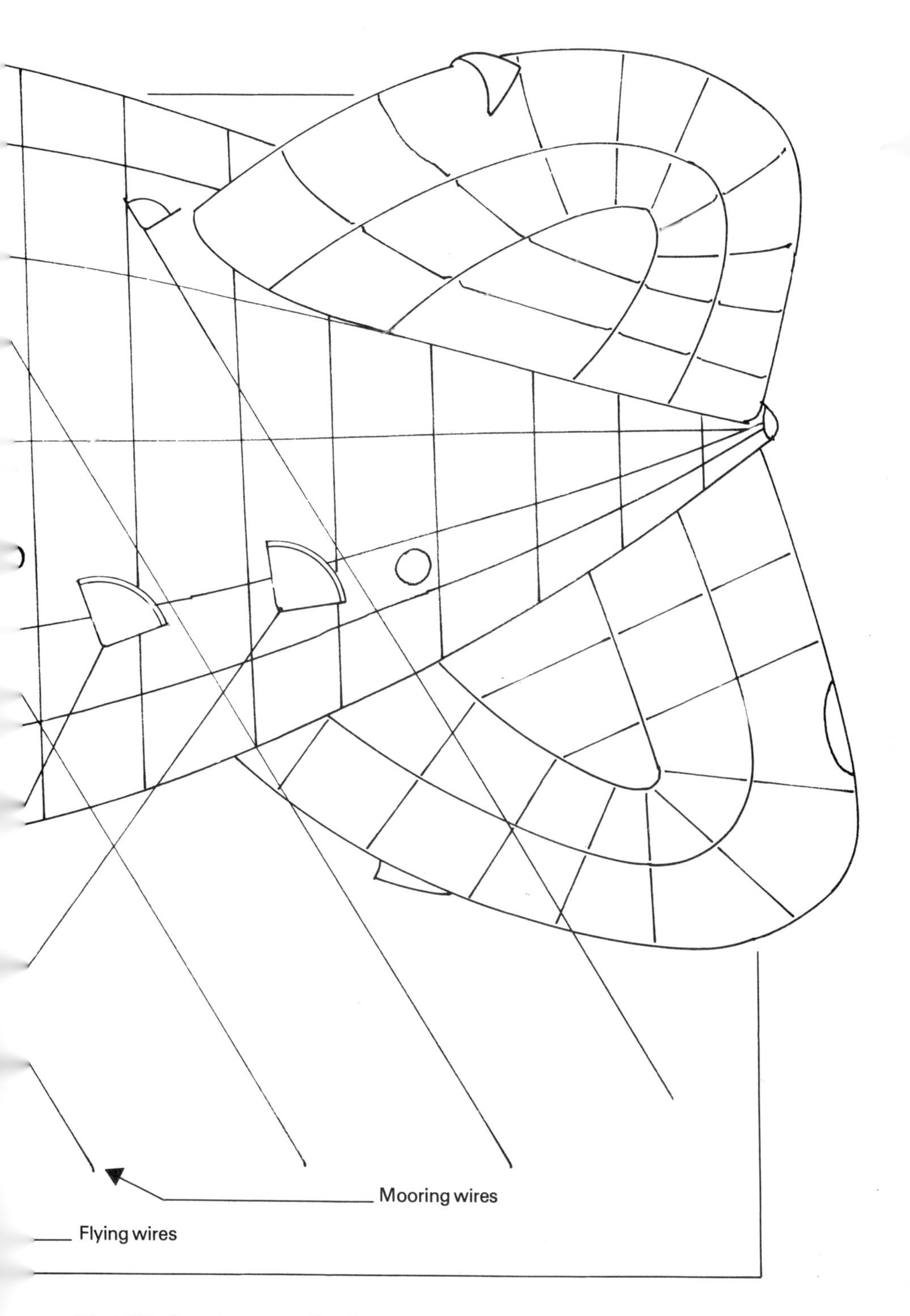
Mooring wires
Flying wires

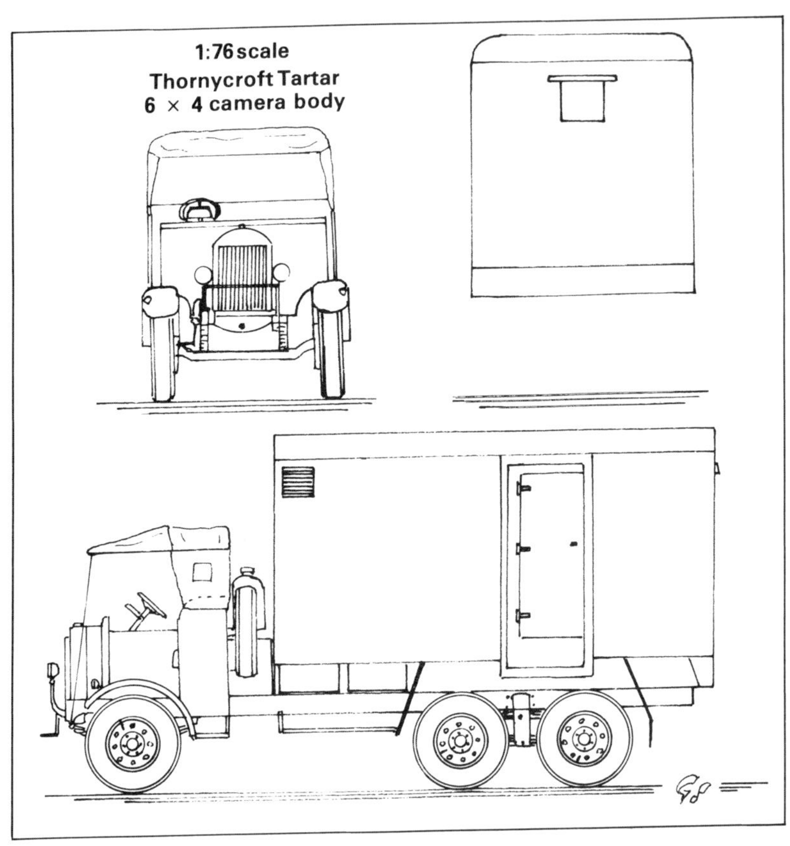

Nice detail shot of barrage balloon—note mooring lines being handled by crew.

characteristic quilted appearance. An aerosol spray of silver/grey paint will complete the effect ready for adding the rigging to an unusual model.

Crossley 1GL8 6 × 4 searchlight

Continuing the defensive theme, the use of searchlights in conjunction with anti-aircraft guns and balloon barrages was about all we had in the way of an answer in the early days of the Blitz. Air defence at night was primitive until radar-equipped guns and aircraft were developed, having to rely on sound detectors and searchlights to pick up the attackers. The Crossley was one of many like the GUY, FBAX and Leyland Retriever used for transporting the tracked portable searchlights to gun sites. See later drawings for the chassis and for the searchlight. The body is fitted with a forward crew compartment, note doors each side, with two bench seats across the full width of the body. Note also the rectangular fuel tank behind the cab on the near side and the spare wheel on the offside. Austin K6 wheels and axles can be used, the rest being as previously described. This chassis was also fitted with a Coles crane (see Leyland Retriever below), a workshop No 4 and GS bodies.

Thornycroft Tartar 6 × 4 camera body

A similar vehicle to the Crossley, this chassis was also fitted with 3-ton GS, wireless and workshop bodies.

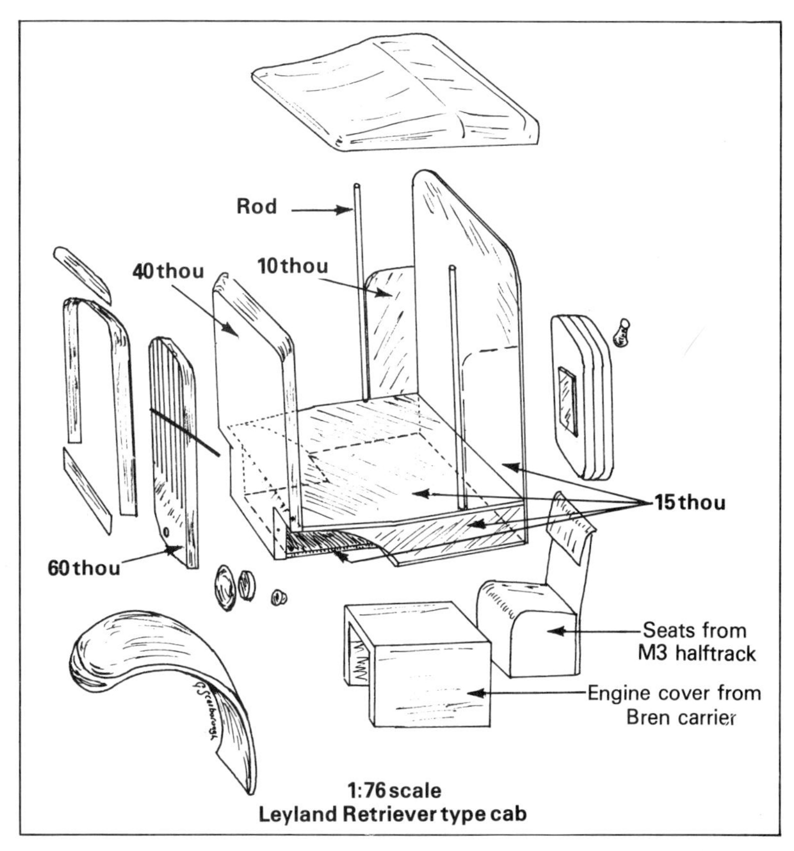

1:76 scale
Leyland Retriever type cab

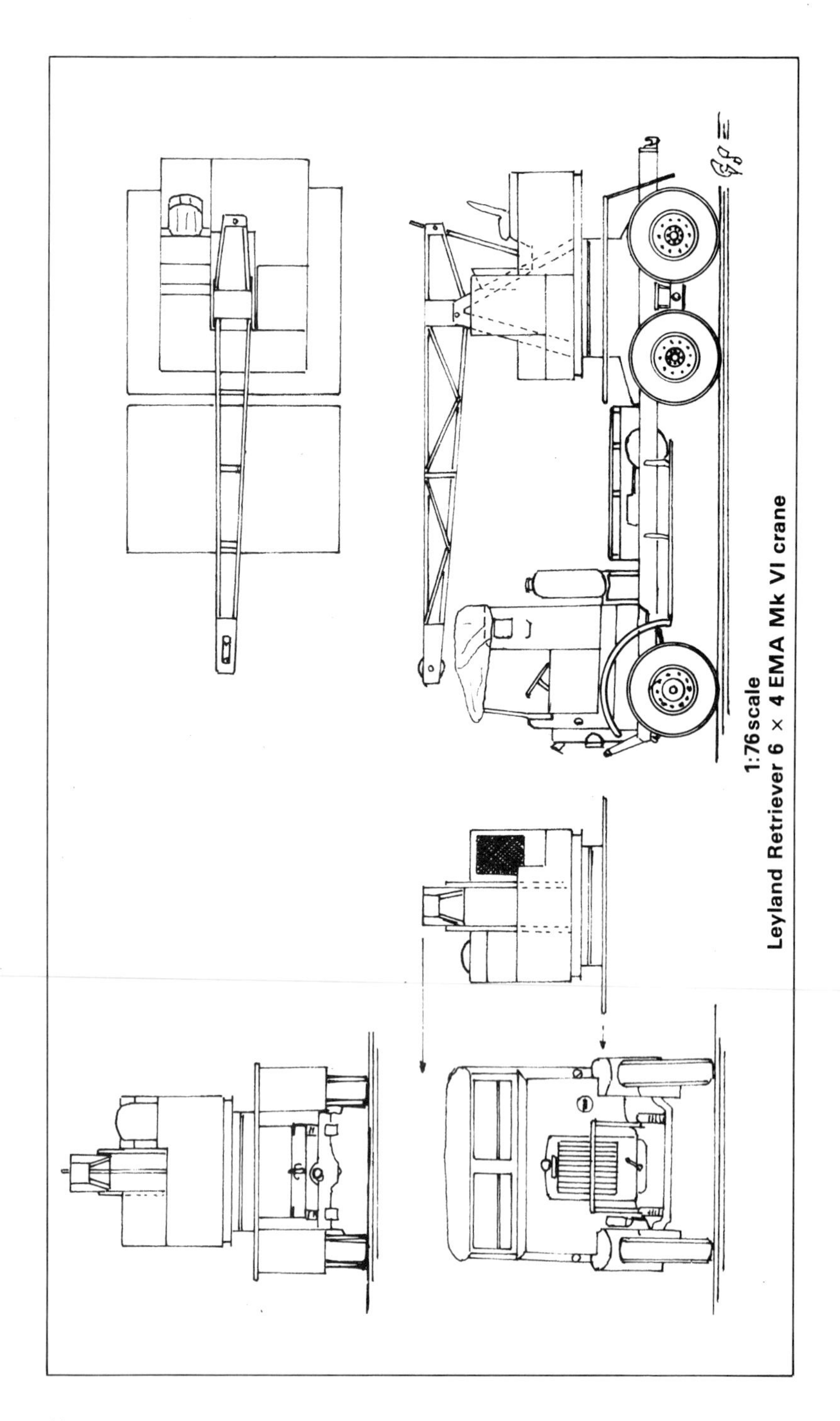

1:76 scale
Leyland Retriever 6 × 4 EMA Mk VI crane

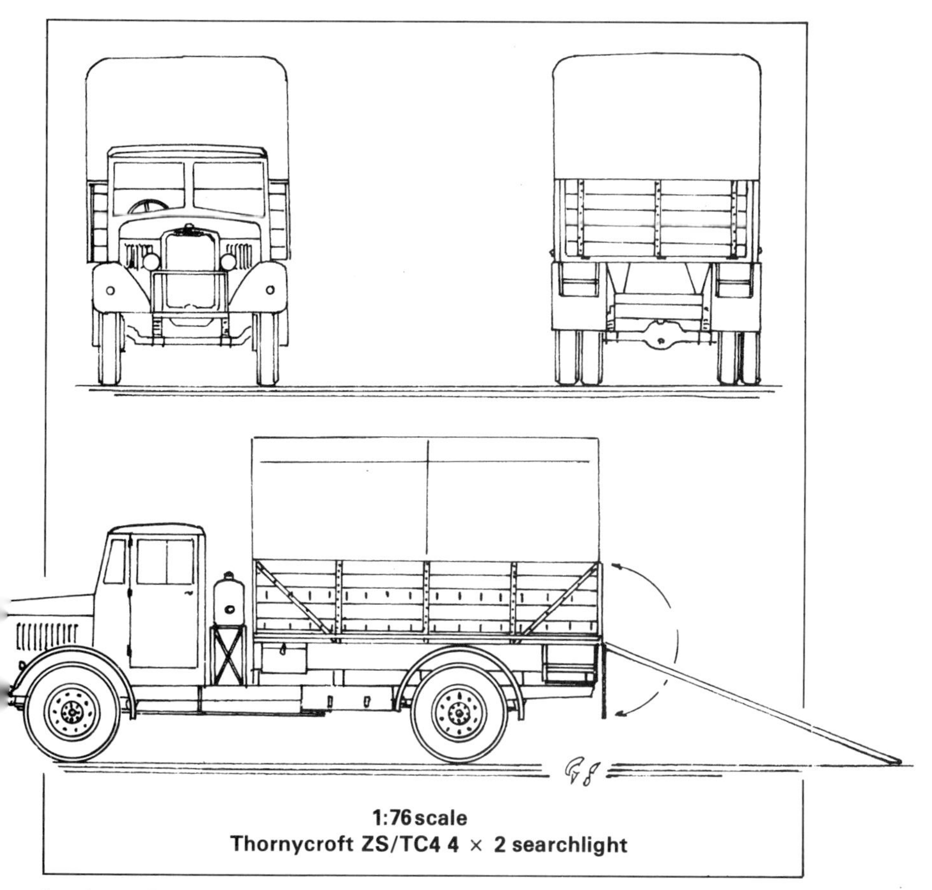

1:76 scale
Thornycroft ZS/TC4 4 × 2 searchlight

Leyland Retriever/Coles crane

Yet another similar chassis which, apart from the crane shown, can be fitted with the camera body, plotter, recorder, printing, machinery, workshop or 3-ton GS.

Thornycroft ZS/TC4 4 × 2 searchlight

One of the smaller type projector transporters, the Thornycroft was fitted with a generator mounted in front of the engine. The loading ramps were carried under the body floor and the model is essentially a GS type truck. Note twin rear wheels, fuel tank behind cab on nearside and spare wheel on offside. Wheels can come from the Austin K6 and the rest is similar to already described.

90 cm Light Projector

I was fortunate to come across two preserved examples of this searchlight in one weekend, the one drawn which is now exhibited at Newark Air Museum, and the other, privately owned, being a similar projector but mounted on a turntable on a two-wheeled pneumatic tyred trailer. Although the little track bogies are badly rotted through standing some 30-odd years in a field, the projector now safe at Newark is otherwise in fair condition. A small model like this does not require a lot of detail but for those interested I have included two of my photographs which

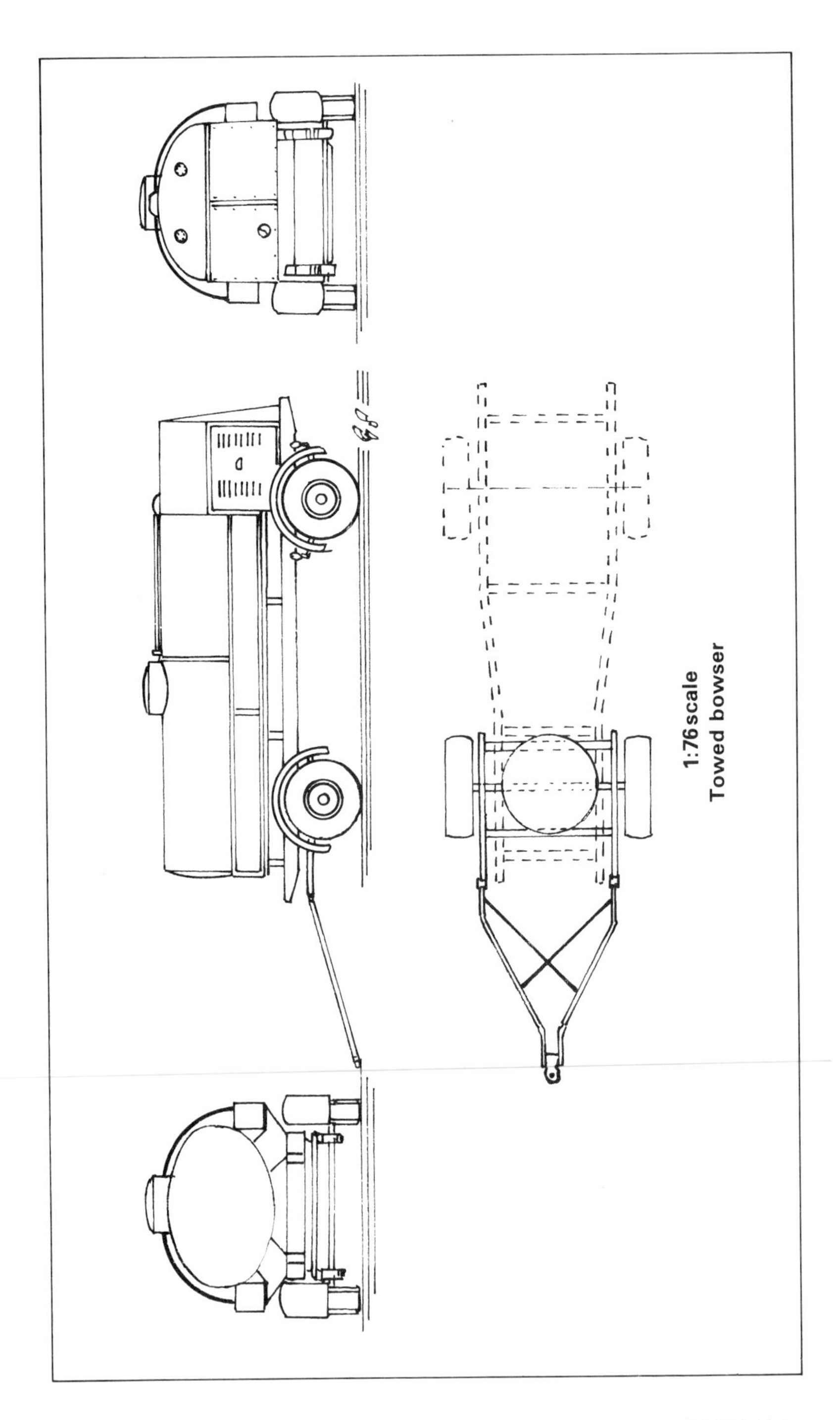

1:76 scale
Towed bowser